RED-TAIL ANGELS

WALKER AND COMPANY ✺ NEW YORK

Red-Tail ANGELS

The Story of the
Tuskegee Airmen of
World War II

PATRICIA AND FREDRICK McKISSACK

Dedicated to
John "Buddy" Petway,
who gave his life in the service of his country

First published in the United States of America in 1995 by Walker Publishing Company, Inc.

Published simultaneously in Canada by Thomas Allen & Son Canada, Limited, Markham, Ontario

Library of Congress Cataloging-in-Publication Data
McKissack, Pat, 1944–
    Red-tail angels : the story of the Tuskegee airmen of World War II / Patricia and Fredrick McKissack.
        p. cm.
    Includes bibliographical references.
    Summary : A history of African-American pilots with a focus on World War II.
    ISBN 0-8027-8292-2 (hardcover). ISBN 0-8027-8293-0 (reinforced) 1. World War, 1939–1945—Aerial operations, American—Juvenile literature. 2. World War, 1939–1945—Participation, Afro-Americans—Juvenile literature. 3. Afro-American air pilots—History—Juvenile literature. 4. Tuskegee Army Air Field (Ala.)—Juvenile Literature. [1. Afro-American air pilots—History. 2. Air pilots—History. 3. World War, 1939–1945—Participation, Afro-American. 4. World War, 1939–1945—Aerial operations, American.]
    I. McKissack, Fredrick. II. Title.
D790.M333 1995
940.54'4973—dc20   95-15223
                                                          CIP
                                                          AC

Photograph on page ii courtesy of the National Air and Space Museum/Smithsonian Institution; photograph on page vii courtesy of Maxwell Air Force Base Archives.

Book design by Diane Stevenson of Snap-Haus Graphics

Printed in the United States of America
10 9 8 7 6 5 4 3 2 1

CONTENTS

AUTHORS' NOTE

A BLACK STUDENT, who was taking a college course in American history, mentioned to her professor that her father had been a pilot during World War II. He assured the student that her father was simply "telling a story to make himself seem important," because there were no black pilots during the war. The student called her father and asked him to send copies of anything he had that would prove he had been a member of the renowned 332nd Fighter Group in the United States Army Air Corps. A package arrived a few days later. Anxiously, the student rushed to her professor's office and confronted him with all the evidence. Although she waited for him to correct his statement about there being no black pilots during World War II, he never did.

When we heard the above story, we were convinced that this book was necessary. We wrote *Red-Tail Angels: The Story of the Tuskegee Airmen of World War II* with joy and enthusiasm, because we learned so much about a part of American history that has not been accurately or completely told. This has not been a project for which we can take full credit because so many people helped us. We'd like to thank Fredrick McKissack, Jr., Robert McKissack, Mary Virginia Carwell, and Moses (Andy) McKissack for organizing, sorting, and reviewing hundreds of seemingly disconnected pieces of information; Bill Rice, who helped with the photo research; Chris Newman, historian of the Hugh White Chapter of the Tuskegee Airmen, St. Louis, who helped us get started; and Joe Caver, Archivist at Maxwell Air Force Base, who helped us finish. For all the assistance we received in between, we especially thank Mrs. Clara White and Mrs. Darien Moten, widows of Tuskegee Airmen, George Carper, Woodrow Crockett, George Davis, III, George Mitchell, and others who willingly shared their hurts and frustrations as well as their joys and triumphs with us. We'd like to express our gratitude to General Benjamin O. Davis, Jr., United States Air Force (retired), with whom we shared a wonderful Sunday brunch and hours of interesting conversation. And, finally, without the patience and persistence of our editor, Emily Easton, this book would not have been possible. Thank you all.

BLACK EAGLES IN FLIGHT

From Tuskegee came these flyers
signed by a black panther
proving skills that took them higher

to break barriers malign.
They earned their wartime wings
over deserts, fields of brine.

Sons of workers, sons of kings,
men to lead, and men to build,
in the air brave spirit awakenings

To the glory they fulfilled
in their mastery of the sky.
New nobility undrilled

revealed a heritage of right,
pushing open doors of flight.

—Carol Washburne, 1994

332d Fighter Group

99th Fighter Squadron

100th Fighter Squadron

301st Fighter Squadron

302d Fighter Squadron

INTRODUCTION

THE STORY OF the Tuskegee Airmen sheds light on the role of African-Americans in the military, an aspect of American history that has been forgotten or marginalized in many textbooks. Today, it is unthinkable that until the end of World War II, African-Americans were not allowed to serve in the United States Air Force. But in fact they were not.

In 1948, President Harry S Truman issued an executive order, which eventually ended segregation in the various United States military branches. Before that time, African-American soldiers were not given the same opportunities as their white counterparts. The records show, however, that black soldiers have been present and accounted for in every major military encounter in either an official or an unofficial capacity since Jamestown, Virginia, the first English settlement in North America.

According to Richard M. Dalfiume, a military scholar and author, it was the practice of colonial leaders to arm blacks "when emergencies, such as Indian threats, arose and there was immediate need for man-power." Slaves and free persons of color were called upon "to defend forts, outposts, and small settlements," but as soon as the crisis ended, they were disarmed immediately and denied the right to participate in the peacetime militia.

The colonists' dilemma was that they needed to arm slaves to fend off attacks by Native Americans but feared that armed slaves would turn on their masters. After the external dangers had ceased, could slave soldiers be returned to slavery? Was it logical to arm an oppressed group to fight in defense of their oppressors? These and other questions regarding the use of blacks in the military remained a concern throughout the colonial period.

During the Revolutionary War the enemy had changed, but whites' attitudes and concerns were the same. George Washington refused to enlist blacks in the Continental Army, but he changed his mind when the British Governor of Virginia, Lord Dunmore, offered to free any slave who fought for the British crown and large numbers of blacks answered his call. The colonies could not afford a slave uprising at the same time they were fighting England, so in the North slaves were promised freedom in exchange for their loyal service to the revolutionary cause. Efforts to enlist blacks in the South were rejected, but they were widely used as auxiliary workers for military construction projects.

Of the more than two hundred thousand soldiers who fought for American independence, approximately five thousand were African-American. They fought in almost every major battle of the war, distinguishing themselves with bravery and loyalty. Even though black soldiers were honored for bravery and given medals for courage during the Revolutionary War, after the war was won, some of them were reenslaved. Even free blacks were forbidden to own guns and were banned from the military.

Within twenty years the country found itself again at war with Great Britain. Many of the same circumstances seemed to be repeated. When General Andrew Jackson needed additional men to help defend New Orleans during the War of 1812, he disregarded official policy and issued a proclamation to the "Free Men of Color of Louisiana," asking them to volunteer in the defense of the country and guaranteeing them payment for service equal to that of the white soldiers. But as soon as the war ended, blacks were barred from the military once again, and it

These black soldiers fought to free themselves and their families from the tyranny of slave dealers. (LIBRARY OF CONGRESS)

wasn't until the Civil War that African-Americans were officially permitted to bear arms in defense of the country.

Early in the Civil War, using black men in the Union army met with wide disapproval, because military leaders feared white volunteers would not serve in an integrated army. Even so, a few renegade generals recruited blacks on the battlefield in order to fill out their ranks. However, with pressure from abolitionists such as Frederick Douglass, who argued that blacks had a right to fight for their own freedom, President Abraham Lincoln reconsidered the policy.

When President Lincoln issued the Emancipation Proclamation in January 1863, freeing all slaves in the rebel states, he also made provisions for the enlistment of blacks in the military. As a result, the celebrated all-black 54th Massachusetts Volunteers Regiment was formed. But to hold down criticism, the War Department insisted that black soldiers be paid less than whites. When the soldiers of the 54th and their white officers protested by refusing to accept their less than commensurate pay, the War Department rescinded the order and all soldiers were paid equally.

The 54th and black members of the other 165 regiments of infantry, cavalry, light and heavy artillery, and engineers fought hard and sustained heavy losses, shattering the claim that African-Americans were too undisciplined to make good soldiers. They earned more than twenty Congressional Medals of Honor. If the volunteers in state units, spies, and medical teams are included in the count, it is estimated that close to 390,000 blacks served during the Civil War—about 10 percent

Members of the famed 9th Cavalry known as the Buffalo Soldiers.

of the Union army—and suffered more than 38,000 fatalities. (Some sources believe the death toll of black soldiers was greater than 68,000, especially if the deaths caused by the lack of equipment, bad medical care, and poor training are figured in the count.)

After the Civil War, the 24th and 25th Infantries and the 9th and 10th Cavalries became *permanent* all-black army units. Neglected by the army, these soldiers were often left to complete duties without enough guns or ammunition. They even had to design and make their own silk embroidered regimental flag. Although they were poorly trained and equipped and their horses and saddles were old, these black soldiers, many of them former slaves, served on the western frontier, protecting farming communities, stagecoaches, mail stations, and train routes. And they did it well.

The Comanche, Kiowa, Apache, Cheyenne, Arapaho, and other Native Americans whom they met in battle, between 1870 and 1896, called them the Buffalo Soldiers because of their courage and strength. By the beginning of the Spanish-American War, the Buffalo Soldiers had earned fourteen Congressional Medals of Honor.

The 9th and 10th Cavalries made history at the charge up San Juan Hill, and the 25th Infantry helped capture the blockhouse that was the key to the Spanish position at the Battle of El Caney.

The first decade of the twentieth century was a troubled period for race relations. As the gulf between whites and blacks widened in the civilian community, politicians again pushed for the elimination of blacks in the regular army. Although African-Americans made up only about 10 percent of the regular army, that number was drastically reduced following the Brownsville Case of 1906.

After serving in the Spanish-American War, the 24th and 25th Infantry regiments served in the Philippines until 1903, when they were ordered back to the states. The 25th was sent to Fort Brown in Brownsville, Texas. Local residents were hostile toward all blacks and were particularly resentful of black servicemen. Every time these soldiers came into town, they were treated with contempt and scorn.

One night a group of Brownsville citizens came to the fort and accused members of the 25th of riding into town and shooting out store windows, killing a civilian, and wounding several others. The public outcry was loud and vicious. "None of us are safe as long as [blacks] have guns," a Texas newspaper warned.

Members of the 25th pleaded not guilty, and there was overwhelming evidence to prove that they could not have been involved in the shoot-out. Their horses had not been ridden, and their guns had not been fired. After a hasty trial army investigators concluded that there was a conspiracy among the men, and 167 of the Buffalo Soldiers were court-martialed and dishonorably discharged.

On November 26, 1906, President Theodore Roosevelt reviewed their appeal and upheld the conviction. The convicted soldiers lost their rank, pensions, and veteran's benefits. One man had served twenty-seven years in the army; twenty-five had served over ten years; six were Medal of Honor winners, and thirteen had citations for bravery in the Spanish-American War.

On September 28, 1972, the records from the Brownsville trial were reviewed by a congressional committee, which recommended that the 167 soldiers be reinstated and given honorable discharges. Dorsey Willis was the only member of the original group still alive and able to benefit from the decision. In 1973 Congress passed a bill that granted Willis twenty-five thousand dollars in compensation and provided him with medical care at a veteran's hospital in Minneapolis until his death.

Given the history of poor treatment in the military, blacks had good reason to avoid military service, but there were always sufficient numbers of blacks who were willing to serve in the army and navy. When the United States entered World War I, African-American leaders, such as W. E. B. Du Bois, encouraged young black men to forget about the internal struggle and "close ranks" with white Americans for the common good of the country. And, once again, 375,000 men—from Mississippi sharecroppers to Chicago English professors—enlisted and served in four all-black units.

Nicknamed the Hell Fighters by the Germans, the men of the celebrated 369th fought in the trenches for 191 days, under heavy fire, yet they never retreated or had a member captured.

At the same time African-Americans were risking their lives to defend democracy, the United States Army issued a memorandum to the French command, asking them to prevent any "pronounced degree of intimacy" between French and African-American soldiers. The memo further requested that the French should not "eat with Negroes, shake hands or seek to meet with them outside of military service." But most of all, the French were asked not "to commend black soldiers too highly in the presence of white Americans."

The French responded by giving the entire 369th Regiment the

Over 200,000 black men served overseas during World War I. Numerous members of the all-black fighting units were honored by the French government for their bravery in battle. (LIBRARY OF CONGRESS)

croix de guerre, a high French military award. And Privates Needham Roberts and Henry Johnson, members of the 369th, were individually decorated with the croix de guerre for their heroism. Soldiers from other black regiments were also awarded honors.

The armistice was signed on November 11, 1918. The "war to end all wars" was over. As was the case in previous wars, proud black soldiers returned home hopeful that their honorable service and outstanding displays of courage and discipline would translate into respect for them at home. But they were wrong.

Despite their performance and character, black soldiers were not accepted or respected by the military or by the civilian communities to which they returned. Preaching hatred and fear, groups such as the reorganized Ku Klux Klan conjured up visions of a well-trained "black army," against which the white race needed to defend itself.

During the summer of 1919 seventy-six blacks were lynched, some of them servicemen still in their uniforms. Whites rioted in twenty-five cities and savagely beat and killed innocent women and children. They burned African-American businesses and schools. Out of the ashes of the "Red Summer" of 1919 emerged a new African-American whose militancy was captured by Claude McKay, a young poet, who wrote "If We Must Die":

> If we must die, let it not be like hogs
> Hunted and penned in an inglorious spot,
> While round us bark the mad and hungry dogs,
> Making their mock at our accursed lot.
> If we must die, O let us nobly die,
> So that our precious blood may not be shed
> In vain; then even the monsters we defy
> Shall be constrained to honor us though dead!
> O kinsmen! we must meet the common foe!

Though far outnumbered let us show us brave,

And for their thousand blows deal one deathblow!

What though before us lies the open grave?

Like men we'll face the murderous, cowardly pack,

Pressed to the wall, dying, but fighting back!

Between the two wars, the Great Depression plunged the nation into an economic abyss. Whites were poor, and blacks were poorer still. The whole economic picture was bleak. Some whites chose military careers because it offered them a way out of their grinding poverty. Black men tried the same avenue of escape, but the peacetime army and navy turned them away.

The army and navy made it clear that they didn't want black volunteers except in menial positions. During the early 1930s, the number of black soldiers in the regular army dwindled to the lowest level since the Civil War. Then when the Army and Navy Air Corps became integral parts of the U.S. military, men of all races and nationalities were drawn to the drama and excitement of airplanes. But African-American men were not admitted to the air divisions because of the prevailing racial attitudes of the civilian population.

The military establishment chose to believe African-Americans were not smart enough or disciplined enough to fly combat aircraft, even though black pilots had distinguished themselves in the French Air Force during World War I. To support their false assumptions, military officials concocted an infamous report issued by the War College in 1925.

The report stated that African-Americans were "a subspecies of the human population" and probably "the worst of all races." It was impossible, in the opinion of the report, for them to be good officers. The army interpreted the report to mean that blacks could not be pilots. The infamous report managed to ignore the accomplishments of black

Black soldiers were reminded of their second-class citizenship by signs like these. (LIBRARY OF CONGRESS)

military heroes and such out-standing pilots as Bessie Coleman, William Powell, Willa Brown, Cornelius Coffey, John C. Robinson, and the World War I flying ace Eugene Bullard (about whom a film was made in 1926 titled *The Flying Ace*). All the assertions in the report were made without one shred of scientific proof, yet it was accepted as truth, until March 1942, when five African-American men earned their silver wings at Tuskegee Army Air Field in Alabama.

These five black pilots were part of an "experiment," designed as a result of pressure put on the War Department by African-American leaders and the press. Their persistent demands for the admission of blacks in the Army Air Corps paid off in early 1941. The secretary of war reluctantly approved a plan to establish the all-black 99th Fighter Squadron and to construct an air base located in Tuskegee, Alabama, where other black pilots could be trained.

The experimental program was designed to fail. But against all odds, young black men from all over the country, most with two years of college or more, proved to a doubtful nation that they could fly air-planes. Then to their dismay, the question became, "How will they fare in combat?" The answer is a matter of history.

By 1946, over 992 black pilots (not including ground crews) had been trained at the segregated facilities at Tuskegee Army Air Field (TAAF). From 1942 until the end of the war, many of these men served in the all-black 332nd Fighter Group, composed of the original 99th, 100th, 301st, and 302nd Fighter Squadrons.

Although the black fighters got off to a shaky start, as they gained confidence they flew hundreds of successful missions over North Africa and Europe, eventually gaining the respect and admiration of the military brass who had questioned their ability and doubted their courage. Known fondly as the Red-Tail Angels because of the red markings on the tails of their aircraft, these pioneer pilots earned a reputation for never losing a bomber they escorted. In addition, they brought home 150 Distinguished Flying Crosses and Legions of Merit. Sixty-six pilots died in aerial combat, defending the rights of others—rights they themselves did not enjoy. But their sacrifices were not in vain.

The accomplishments of the Tuskegee pilots, navigators, and crewmen helped defeat Nazi tyranny and set an inspiring example of courage and competence to people around the world, and in so doing hastened the end of segregation in the military and in civilian society.

Members of the 15th Air Force, 332nd Fighter Group, 100th Fighter Squadron, in Italy during World War II. (L to R) Lt. Dempsey Morgan, Lt. Carroll Woods, Lt. Robert Nelson, Jr., Capt. Andrew D. Turner (the commanding officer of the 100th and beneath whose P-51 Mustang, Skipper's Darlin', the group is posed), and Lt. Clarence "Lucky" Lester. (NATIONAL AIR AND SPACE MUSEUM/SMITHSONIAN INSTITUTION)

ONE

1900–1939

FLYING BECOMES A REALITY

As FAR BACK AS anyone can trace, human beings have dreamed of flying. Ancient myths about half-human/half-bird creatures are plentiful. Birds were—and continue to be—symbols of freedom, power, and majesty. History is also filled with true stories about people who risked their lives and reputations trying to fly. Some of these first adventurers sought to become airborne by attaching wings to their arms and flapping frantically. The Chinese studied wind currents and flew for short distances on gliders. Leonardo da Vinci, a true genius of the Renaissance, left drawings and a theory of flying that was remarkably scientific for his era. Others built complicated contraptions that puttered, fluttered, and sputtered before collapsing into dramatic failure. The development of hot-air balloons was a major event in aviation history, inspiring both romantic notions of endless wandering (Jules Verne's *Around the World in Eighty Days*) and military strategies to check enemy positions during times of war.

For most people this preoccupation with flying was viewed as a ridiculous waste of time: Humans were not supposed to fly. For others, however, the unrelenting pressure of their dreams forced them to keep

Wilbur (l) and Orville (r) Wright with their sister, Katherine, November 4, 1909. (Library of Congress)

trying. Then, building on the science of physicists, the technology of engineers, and the hope of a few dreamers, two brothers—owners of a bicycle shop in Dayton, Ohio—made a quantum leap in aviation on December 17, 1903. On that historic morning Orville Wright, with the assistance of his brother Wilbur, sailed off Kill Devil Hill at Kitty Hawk, North Carolina, in a heavier-than-air, power-driven machine, later to be called an airplane. The flights—there were four that day—lasted less than a minute, but this was the beginning of a new era in science and technology.

Three years later, Alberto Santos-Dumont, a Brazilian living in France, became the first person to fly a biplane in Europe. On July 25, 1909, Louis Blériot piloted a plane of his own design across the English Channel from France to England. In less than ten years after the Wright brothers' breakthrough, aviation had become a reality for both military and sporting purposes.

It is interesting to note that flying an airplane became a reality at a time when most Americans had not yet seen an automobile and were still dependent on the horse and buggy as a basic means of transportation. For the average person who dared to dream of flying, the possibility must have seemed even more remote than living one day on a starship might seem to us today. Yet people did dream, regardless of age, regardless of sex, regardless of race.

WOMEN IN AVIATION

AMERICAN AVIATION WAS from its very beginnings marred with sexist and racist assumptions. It was taken for granted that women were generally inferior to men and that white men were superior to all others. Flying, it was said, required a level of skill and courage that women and blacks lacked. Yet despite these prevailing prejudices, the dream and the desire to fly stayed alive among women and African-Americans.

The story of women in aviation actually goes back to the time of the hot-air balloons. A number of women in Europe and America gained fame for their skill and daring. Sophie Blanchard made her first solo balloon flight in 1805. She grew in fame and was eventually named official aeronaut of the empire by Napoleon. By 1834, at least twenty women in Europe were piloting their own balloons.

Though she did not fly, Katherine Wright was a major supporter of her brothers' efforts. Orville so appreciated his sister's help that he said, "When the world speaks of the Wrights, it must include my sister. . . . She inspired much of our effort."

Although Raymonde de la Roche of France was the first woman in the world to earn her pilot's license, Harriet Quimby held the distinction of being the first American woman to become a licensed pilot.

On August 1, 1911, Quimby, who was described as a "real beauty" with "haunting blue-green eyes," strolled off the field after passing her

Harriet Quimby was the first American woman to earn her pilot's license. (NATIONAL AIR AND SPACE MUSEUM/SMITHSONIAN INSTITUTION)

pilot's test easily. To the male reporters who inundated her with questions, Quimby fired back answers with self-confidence. Walking past a group of women who had come to witness the historic event, Quimby was overheard to quip with a smile and a wink: "Flying is easier than voting." (The Woman's Suffrage Amendment wasn't passed until 1920.)

As difficult as it was for women to become pilots in significant numbers, it was doubly hard for African-Americans, especially black women. That's why Bessie Coleman, the first African-American to earn her pilot's license, is such an exciting and important figure in aviation.

Bessie Coleman was born in 1893 in Atlanta, Texas, the twelfth of thirteen children. Her mother, who had been a slave, valued education and encouraged all of her children to attend school in order to better themselves. The encouragement paid off, because Coleman graduated from high school, a feat not too many black women were able to accomplish in the early 1900s.

Bessie Coleman refused to accept the limitations others tried to place on her. She attended an Oklahoma college for one semester but ran out of money. Accepting the offer of one of her brothers to come live with him and his family in Chicago, Coleman found a job as a manicurist. She fully intended to return to school after saving enough money. But she never did. While in Chicago she learned about flying and made a new set of goals for herself. She wanted to be a pilot.

Coleman learned about flying from reading newspaper accounts of air battles during World War I. She tried to find a school that would accept her as a trainee. But no American instructor or flying school was willing to teach her.

When the war ended, a friend, Robert S. Abbott, the founder of the *Chicago Defender*, one of the most popular black-owned and -operated newspapers in the country, suggested that Coleman go to France, where racial prejudice was not as restrictive as it was in America. Even though the United States was the birthplace of flight, it was slower than other countries to develop an organized aviation program. European leaders immediately saw the commercial and military advantages of a strong national aviation program. Bessie knew from her reading that both French and German aircraft were among the best in the world.

Coleman had also read about Eugene Jacques Bullard, the well-decorated and highly honored native of Georgia who had become the first African-American to fly an airplane in combat as a member of the French Lafayette Flying Corps during World War I. Other blacks had gone to Europe to get their training, too. Coleman realized that if she were ever going to get a chance to fly, she, too, would have to go to France. But she didn't have any money to get there, and besides, she couldn't speak a word of French.

Bessie Coleman, the first African-American woman pilot, inspired thousands with her courage and skill. (NATIONAL AIR AND SPACE MUSEUM/SMITHSONIAN INSTITUTION)

Eugene Jacques Bullard flew in the French air force during World War I. (National Air and Space Museum/Smithsonian Institution)

For almost two years, Coleman worked part-time as a manicurist and as a server in a Chicago chili parlor and saved every penny to finance her trip to France. Meanwhile she learned to speak French, so when the time came, she'd be able to understand her instructors.

In 1921, Coleman made it to France, where she

Bessie Coleman's French pilot's license issued on June 15, 1921. (National Air and Space Museum/Smithsonian Institution) found an instructor who was one of Tony Fokker's chief pilots. Fokker, the famous aircraft manufacturer, said Coleman was a "natural talent." On June 15, 1921, Coleman made history by becoming the first black woman to earn her wings, thus joining the ranks of the handful of American women fliers.

Returning to the United States determined to start a flying school where other African-American pilots could be trained, Coleman looked for ways to finance her dream. There were very few jobs in the aviation industry for women or blacks. She soon learned that there was little or no support for a black woman who wanted to start a flying school. To call attention to aviation and to encourage other women and African-Americans to take part in the new and growing field, Coleman gave flying exhibitions and lectured on aviation. She thrilled audiences with her daredevil maneuvers, just as Quimby had done before her.

Along with racism, Coleman encountered the burden of sexism, but she made believers out of those who doubted her skill. "The color of my skin," she said, "[was] a drawback at first. . . . I was a curiosity, but soon the public discovered I could really fly. Then they came to see *Brave Bessie*, as they called me."

The strict rules and regulations that govern aviation today didn't exist during the first three decades of flying. For example, it wasn't uncommon for aviators to ignore safety belts and fly without parachutes. One of these simple safety precautions might have saved the lives of both Harriet Quimby and Bessie Coleman.

On a July morning in 1912, Quimby, and a passenger named William P. Willard, set out to break an over-water speed record. When Quimby climbed to five thousand feet, the French-made Blériot monoplane suddenly nosed down. Both Quimby and Willard were thrown from the plane and plunged to their deaths in the Boston Harbor.

The *New York Sun* used the opportunity to speak out against women fliers:

Miss Quimby is the fifth woman in the world killed while operating an aeroplane (three were students) and their number thus far is five too many. The sport is not one for which women are physically qualified. As a rule they lack strength and presence of mind and the courage to excel as aviators. It is essentially a man's sport and pastime.

Fourteen years later, Bessie Coleman died in a similar accident. With almost enough savings to start her school, Coleman agreed to do an air show in Florida on May Day for the Negro Welfare League of Jacksonville. At 7:30 P.M. the night before, Coleman, accompanied by her publicity agent, William Wills, took her plane up for a test flight. When she reached an altitude of about five thousand feet, her plane flipped over. Coleman was thrown from the plane and plunged to her death April 30, 1926. Wills died seconds later when the plane crashed.

Once again critics used the tragedy to assert that neither women nor blacks were mentally or physically able to be good pilots. "Women are often penalized by publicity for their every mishap," said Amelia

Earhart, the most famous female pilot in aviation history. "The result is that such emphasis sometimes directly affects [a woman's] chances for a flying job," Earhart continued. "I had one manufacturer tell me that he couldn't risk hiring women pilots because of the way accidents, even minor ones, became headlines in the newspapers."

Although Bessie Coleman died tragically, her plans to open a flight training school for blacks were continued by those she had inspired.

Amelia Earhart (1887–1937) was the first woman to fly across the Atlantic Ocean. This 8-cent stamp was issued in her honor by the U.S. Post Office, July 24, 1963.

During the early 1930s, William Powell founded the Bessie Coleman Flying Schools in California. He encouraged African-Americans to become active in the growing aviation industry. (NATIONAL AIR AND SPACE MUSEUM/SMITHSONIAN INSTITUTION)

BLACK FLYING CLUBS

BY THE LATE 1920S and the early 1930s, Chicago and Los Angeles had become centers of black aviation. In California, William Powell, himself a pilot, founded the Bessie Coleman Flying Schools to honor this aviation pioneer. Club members learned how to fly for fun and sport. But Powell also encouraged them to become more involved in the business aspects of aviation. *Black Wings*, a journal published by Powell, featured articles about the business opportunities flying offered. He encouraged professional blacks to pool their talents and resources and start commercial airlines, build airports, and design and manufacture aircraft.

The reality, of course, was that without equality of opportunity and a strong financial base, blacks' ability to compete successfully for jobs and training in this growing industry was only a dream. Yet Powell's forward-thinking ideas inspired black people to keep trying.

In 1931, the National Association for the Advancement of Colored People (NAACP) wrote a letter to the War Department requesting that African-American men be accepted into the Army Air Corps. The department replied, "The colored man had not been attracted to flying in the same way or to the extent of the white man" and that it had received so many applications from college-trained white men that many white applicants had to be turned down.

Walter White, secretary of the NAACP, responded:

It is obvious that colored men cannot be attracted to the field of aviation in the same way or to the same extent as the white man, when the door to that field is slammed in the colored man's face. . . . There are thousands of excellent colored mechanics in the country and if the War Department did not prejudice the case by definitely excluding them, we feel sure that there would be no difficulty in finding and developing men with all the qualifications required of pilots, mechanics, and all the other functions included in the air service.

Members of the Challenger Air Pilots Association located in Chicago, 1933. Members included Willa Brown, her husband, Cornelius Coffey, and founder, John Robinson (far right). (NATIONAL AIR AND SPACE MUSEUM/SMITHSONIAN INSTITUTION)

Cornelius Coffey (center) and members of the Coffey School of Aeronautics. (NATIONAL AIR AND SPACE MUSEUM/SMITHSONIAN INSTITUTION)

In Chicago, 1931, John C. Robinson and a group of men and women air enthusiasts helped organize the Challenger Air Pilots' Association, also inspired by the legacy of Bessie Coleman. When white airstrips refused to allow the Challengers to use their facilities, they bought land in 1932, in the all-black community of Robbins, Illinois, and built their own airstrip.

Two other persons who had a tremendous impact on black aviation were the husband-and-wife team of Willa Brown and Cornelius Coffey. Brown received a masters degree from Northwestern University in education, and she held a master's mechanics certificate and a commercial pilot's rating. Coffey was a member of the first all-black class of aircraft mechanics graduating from the Curtiss-Wright Aeronautical School in 1931. Brown and Coffey established the Coffey School of Aeronautics at Harlem Airport where the Challengers, whose airstrip had been destroyed by a windstorm, were stationed.

The Harlem Airport, located on the southwest side of Chicago, was the site of spectacular air shows during the 1930s. Stunt pilots such as Willie "Suicide" Jones, Dorothy Darby, Harold Hurd, Herbert Julian, and Chauncey E. Spencer thrilled audiences with their skillfully executed aerobatics. And in 1932, James Herman Banning and Thomas C. Allen, the Flying Hobos, made history when they completed a flight across the United States in forty-one hours, twenty-seven minutes.

In 1936, Robinson organized a group of flyers also known as the

Top left:
Harold Hurd, member of the first all-black class to graduate from Curtiss-Wright Aeronautical School. He became an officer in the Army Air Force during World War II. (NATIONAL AIR AND SPACE MUSEUM/SMITHSONIAN INSTITUTION)

Middle:
Herbert Julian, a flamboyant stunt pilot, during the 1930s. (NATIONAL AIR AND SPACE MUSEUM/SMITHSONIAN INSTITUTION)

Below:
J. Herman Banning and Thomas C. Allen made the first coast-to-coast flight in 1932. (NATIONAL AIR AND SPACE MUSEUM/SMITHSONIAN INSTITUTION)

FIRST TRANS-CONTINENTAL FLIGHT

Challengers. They went to Africa to train members of the Ethiopian Air Force. When fascist Italy invaded Ethiopia, Robinson and his men barely escaped.

Charles "Chief" Anderson deserves recognition for being one of the first black aviation businessmen. He was an experienced pilot and master instructor, and an inspiration to all those who came under his influence. He bought his first plane in 1928 for three thousand dollars and earned his commercial pilot's license in 1932. Anderson and Dr. A. Forsythe were the first blacks to complete a transcontinental, round-trip flight in 1933, flying from Atlantic City to Los Angeles and back in a Fairchild 24 cabin monoplane, *The Pride of Atlantic City*. The following year the Anderson-Forsythe team conducted a Pan-American air tour; their Lambert Monocoupe, named *The Spirit of Booker T. Washington*, touched down in Cuba, Jamaica, Haiti, and six other Caribbean countries.

By 1939, Anderson defied all odds and started a commercial air service from a seaplane based on the Potomac River in Washington, D.C.,

Charles Anderson (l) standing next to Dr. Alfred E. Forsythe before one of their Pan-American Goodwill Flights, which took place in 1933 and 1934. They are standing next to the airplane they called The Spirit of Booker T. Washington. (NATIONAL AIR AND SPACE MUSEUM/SMITHSONIAN INSTITUTION)

25

and a land plane facility from a field in nearby Virginia. To put Anderson's achievements in perspective, one of his biographers noted: "In 1939 a grand total of 125 black Americans held licenses as pilots: four commercial, four limited commercial and 23 private, and 94 amateur students."

According to a display at the Air Force Museum in Dayton, Ohio, between 1903 to 1939, airplane construction went from mostly wood and fabric to "internally braced monoplanes, with retractable landing gear, flaps, variable pitch propellers, and enclosed cabins." And just as William Powell and others had predicted, airplane service and manufacturing by 1940 had become a booming industry. A network of jobs opened up in management, service, and labor, but African-Americans were, for the most part, excluded. In the words of one authority, civilian aviation was "the most racially restrictive" of all the transportation industries. The military offered even fewer opportunities.

THE WAR COLLEGE REPORT

SINCE THERE WAS a rising interest in the Army Air Corps among blacks, the War College prepared a report, issued October 30, 1925, and titled "The Use of Negro Manpower in War." Sent to the chief of staff, the report was the result of "several years' study by the faculty and student body of the Army War College," and signed by Major General H. E. Ely, the War College commandant. It stated that black men felt inferior to whites and were by nature subservient. It further stated that neither white nor black soldiers had any confidence in a black officer, and, in summary, all black men were labeled "inferior human beings." The writers went on to declare blacks were not honest or trustworthy. "Petty thieving, lying, and promiscuity are much more common among Negroes than among whites. Atrocities connected with white women have been the cause of considerable trouble among Negroes." The report placed in question the courage of blacks as well. "In physical courage, it must be admitted that the American Negro falls well back of the white man and possibly behind all other races."

As with most reports of this kind, the conclusions it reached were identical to the racist assumptions that it began with. In addition to defaming blacks, the War College also succeeded in documenting its own racism. However, the report was accepted as truth and was used to block black participation in the Army Air Corps and to account for the absence of high-ranking military officers in the army and navy at that time.

Colonel Charles Young and Colonel Benjamin O. Davis, Sr., were among the very few black officers above the rank of sergeant during the 1920s and 1930s. Colonel Young, one of three nineteenth-century West Point graduates, was forced into retirement just after being recommended for promotion to general.

Colonel Benjamin O. Davis, Sr., had entered the army as a first lieutenant during the Spanish-American War in 1898. He'd served in the all-black 8th Infantry and, later, in the Philippines, Liberia, and Wyoming. Like most black officers at that time, Colonel Davis had spent most of his career teaching military science at all-black colleges, including Wilberforce University in Ohio and the Tuskegee Institute in Alabama.

When Colonel Davis's son, Benjamin O. Davis, Jr., announced that he wanted to go to West Point, his father was proud but also concerned. He understood better than most the kind of racism that his son would encounter in the military academy at West Point.

CADET BENJAMIN O. DAVIS, JR.

BENJAMIN O. DAVIS, JR., grew up an army brat, the son of a career soldier. "My father was all Army through and through," the younger Davis remembered in his autobiography. "I was reared by a soldier to be a soldier." That's why nobody was surprised when Ben Junior wanted to attend West Point Military Academy. Yet no African-American had graduated from West Point in the twentieth century.

The first hurdle Davis had to clear was getting an appointment. Then, as now, U.S. military academy cadets were selected from every state by their congressional representative. Davis was confident, mature, a good student, physically strong, and dedicated to military service. Other young black men had the same qualifications, yet they hadn't been appointed. But circumstances were different this time. There was a black man in the U.S. House of Representatives. Oscar De-Priest had been elected congressman from the South Side of Chicago, in 1928, the first African-American to hold that office since 1901.

In a carefully orchestrated plan, Ben Davis's parents sent him to live on the South Side of Chicago in order to establish residency so DePriest could legally appoint him. For a year, Davis studied at the University of Chicago and used his spare time to prepare for the rigorous entrance examination he would be required to take once his appointment was made.

After several attempts to disqualify him, Davis finally met all the requirements and was ordered to report to "the Point" on July 1, 1932, the same year the U.S. economy plummeted to an all-time low and Franklin D. Roosevelt was elected president of the United States.

The first obstacle had been overcome, but the real challenge lay ahead. Davis was not naive enough to believe there was any advantage in being the only black cadet at "the Point." With regard to bigotry and discrimination, the records of the U.S. military academies at Annapolis and West Point were almost unsurpassed. Between 1870 and 1889, when there were African-Americans in Congress, there were twenty-two blacks appointed. Only twelve passed the entrance examination, and only three men graduated.

28

In June 1870, the first two black cadets arrived at West Point, but within a month only one, James Smith, remained. In a letter to a friend, cadet Smith wrote:

Dear Friend:

. . . I passed the examination all right but my companion Howard was rejected. Since he went away I have been lonely indeed. These fellows appear to be trying their utmost to run me off, and I fear they will succeed. We went into camp yesterday, and all night they were around my tent cursing and swearing at me so that I did not sleep two hours. It is just the same at the table, and what I get to eat I must snatch for like a dog. . . .

I have borne insult upon insult until I am completely worn out. I wish I had some good news for you, but alas! it seems to be getting worse and worse.

Smith endured four miserable years in the academy, but at the end, a bigoted professor failed him in philosophy, which resulted in Smith's dismissal one course short of graduation.

Five other cadets were driven out of West Point before Henry Ossian Flipper finally graduated in 1877. Hostility against him was so widespread, Flipper was accused in 1881 of embezzling government funds. Although he was found innocent of the charges, he was still dismissed from military service and all his appeals were repeatedly denied.

Henry O. Flipper, the first African-American cadet to graduate from West Point in 1877. (United States Military Academy Archives at West Point)

While Lieutenant Flipper was fighting his case, cadet Johnson Chestnut Whittaker was found in his room with his feet bound to the bedstead and his hands tied behind his back. His hair had been chopped off and his ears slashed. Whittaker was court-martialed and found guilty of perpetuating a hoax. Chester Arthur, president of the United States, reviewed the case in 1882 and agreed that the evidence against Whittaker was insubstantial. Still, the officers who had accused Whittaker of inflicting the wounds on himself later formed the committee that ruled to dismiss him anyway.

Two other black cadets endured similar insults and attacks, yet managed to graduate in 1887 and in 1889. But even after graduation, life in the military, which is difficult even in the best of situations, was made almost intolerable by blatant racism and endless harassment. Charles Young, the most well known of the three nineteenth-century graduates, became one of the highest-ranking officers in the army in the early 1900s.

After West Point, Lieutenant Young served in the 10th Cavalry. During the Spanish-American War, he was promoted to major and was cited

for his bravery for leading the 9th Ohio Regiment up San Juan Hill. In 1916, Young was promoted to Lieutenant Colonel. He was later awarded the Spingarn Medal by the NAACP for his efforts in helping to stabilize the frontiers of Liberia. (Liberia was founded by a group of white abolitionists and African-Americans who wanted to create an African homeland for freed slaves.)

Colonel Charles Young, graduate of West Point, 1889. He spent his entire career in the military but died before attaining the rank of general. (UNITED STATES MILITARY ACADEMY ARCHIVES AT WEST POINT)

When it was rumored that General John "Black Jack" Pershing was recommending Colonel Young for a promotion to general, the army retired Young on the grounds of poor health. Young suffered from a variety of ailments, but none serious enough to make him unfit for duty. In a dramatic effort to prove that he was physically able to serve, Young rode on horseback from his home in Ohio to Washington, D.C., a grueling journey of over five hundred miles. But the army would not rescind its order. During World War I, when the military could have used his knowledge and experience, the army recalled Colonel Young to duty four days before the end of the war. He died at the age of fifty-eight, January 8, 1922, in Lagos, Nigeria, never having been promoted to general.

Benjamin Davis, Jr., felt a kinship with all the black men who had gone before him at West Point. He fully expected his stay there to be difficult, too, but he was not prepared for the hypocrisy he encountered.

Cadet Davis noticed right away that he had no roommate. When he asked why, he was told that cadets chose their roommates voluntarily, and that no cadet wanted to share a room with him. Later, Davis learned from correspondence in his files that the decision had been made by the school administration and the cadets were never given an opportunity to choose him as a roommate.

Aside from dealing with the stress of being a "plebe" (first-year student at the academy), Davis also had to suffer the same kind of racial animosity the nineteenth-century black cadets had endured. He, too, found the situation hypocritical as well as frustrating. In his autobiography, Davis cited a section from *Bugle Notes*, a small booklet given to all new cadets, which stated:

> Everyone [at West Point] begins on the same basis for there is no distinction except merit. Money is nothing; character, conduct, and capacity everything. In this respect West Point is truly the greatest democratic institution in existence.

Davis explained: "In my idealism I respected these principles and believed they were worth striving for, even though they apparently did not extend to blacks."

Although it was a less than perfect situation, Davis soon settled in. Then one evening he was lying on his bed when someone knocked on his door and whispered there was going to be a meeting in the sinks (the basement) in ten minutes. He dressed quickly and hurried to the basement, but stopped short when he heard someone say, "What are we going to do about the nigger?"

From that meeting on, cadet Davis became an invisible person. He was *silenced*, which meant none of his classmates spoke to him outside the classroom. Silencing was a form of punishment usually used to force dishonorable cadets to resign. But Davis hadn't done anything wrong, so he refused to buckle under the pressure. Besides, he thought, once the students and faculty realized that he could not be driven away, the harassment would end. It was mistaken optimism on his part.

The months progressed, and the silencing continued. Except for classes, he had no social contact with anyone. The loneliness was dreadful. But he was determined not to let go of his dreams.

"At no time did I consciously show that I was hurt," Davis wrote. "I took solace in the fact that I was mature enough to live through anything other people might submit me to, particularly people I considered to be misguided. I kept telling myself that I was superior in character to them, even to the point of feeling sorry for them; instead I bolstered my feelings by thinking that they were missing a great deal by not knowing me."

After the first year, when he had survived the ordeal, many of his classmates shook his hand and said how much they admired his courage and strength. But in the fall, the silencing continued, and it lasted throughout his remaining three years at West Point.

"To this day," Davis wrote in his autobiography, "I cannot understand how the officials at West Point and the individual cadets, with their continually and vociferously stated belief in *Duty, Honor, and Country* as a way of life, could rationalize their treatment of me."

Through the years some of his classmates have insisted that what Davis called "silencing" was actually the exercise of the right to choose one's friends. "Perhaps the absence of a 'legal' silencing in my case eased their consciences," said Davis, whose story has been documented many times by those who were there and saw what happened. "There was an all-out effort to force me into resignation," said Davis, "and that is an undisputed fact."

Then, to add insult to injury, Davis applied for the Army Air Corps in his senior year, but he was declined, with the patronizing suggestion that he might be happier going to law school. The cloud of the War College report still hung heavy over blacks in the military. The year Davis graduated there were only 6,500 blacks in the army out of a total of 360,000 men. Though they were 10 percent of the civilian population, blacks made up less than 2 percent of the army population.

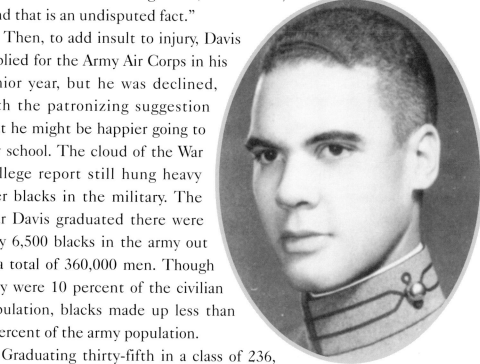

Graduating thirty-fifth in a class of 236, Lieutenant Benjamin Davis, Jr., was not sorry to leave behind the orders, the routine, and the lonely silence he had endured for four years. "There were a lot of people who supported

Cadet Benjamin O. Davis, Jr., West Point class of 1936.
(UNITED STATES MILITARY ACADEMY ARCHIVES AT WEST POINT)

you," Colonel Davis told his son. Lieutenant Davis responded, "It's a pity none of them were at West Point!"

Lieutenant Davis married his sweetheart, Agatha Scott, in the West Point chapel immediately following graduation in 1936, and the newly-weds went to his first assignment at Fort Benning in Georgia. For the next few years, Lieutenant Davis served at several military posts before being assigned to Tuskegee Institute in Alabama, where he taught military science. He was disappointed with the direction his career was taking and was certain he would spend the bulk of it in obscurity.

WAR TALK

BY 1939, GERMANY and Italy had amassed great armies, and Europe was bracing itself for the possibility of war. The U.S. government continued to take a neutral stance. Black and white Americans, eager to fight against what they believed was a threat to world peace and security, volunteered to serve in the Abraham Lincoln Battalion of the International Brigade to defend the Spanish republic. Among those volunteers was James Peck, an African-American from Pittsburgh, who earned recognition as a pilot in Spain. He returned to the United States after four months of battle and went straight to the Army Air Corps Headquarters to brief army intelligence about his experiences.

Peck warned the command that the new German pursuit planes he'd encountered while flying in Spain were superior to the American-made Curtiss P-40s. Peck was immediately ushered out the backdoor. Racism blinded the officers to the fact that Peck was no ordinary pilot but an "ace," meaning he had five victories to his credit. In that day and time, though, Peck's boldness was considered "impertinent."

Full-scale war broke out on September 1, 1939, when fifteen hundred German aircraft invaded Poland. It was the first time an air force had been used to invade a country. A few days later in a Labor Day radio broadcast, President Franklin D. Roosevelt stated that the United States would remain neutral. "I have said not once but many times," the president assured the nation, "that I give you my assurance and reassurance that every effort of your government will be directed to that end."

Even so, by the end of the month Roosevelt had issued an executive agreement granting Britain fifty destroyers in return for a ninety-nine-year rent-free lease for naval and air bases in Newfoundland, Bermuda, the Bahamas, and several other sites.

According to a Gallup Poll, 62 percent of the American public agreed with the president that it was in the nation's best interest to help England in its efforts against Germany. But a group known as the America Firsters, among them the celebrated hero of aviation, Charles Lindbergh, called aid to Britain "interventionism" and warned that such action would eventually drag the United States into war.

Meanwhile, Roosevelt's military advisers were counseling him to prepare the nation for war by increasing the buildup of arms, reinstituting the draft, and vigorously building aircraft. Part of Roosevelt's war readiness plan included the organization of the Civilian Pilot Training Program (CPTP) of the Civil Aeronautics Authority (CAA), which authorized the flight training of twenty thousand college students per year. The reasoning was that these civilian pilots could be adapted to military flying in case war broke out and the army needed to increase the air service quickly.

When it was announced that the CPTP would make use of existing facilities in those institutions which, according to government guidelines, were equipped "to teach the seventy-two-hour ground course and the 35 to 50 hours of flight instruction required for a private flying license," African-Americans insisted that black schools be included in the programs.

To fight for their rights and provide a nationwide organization for black aviators, Willa Brown and others had formed the National Airmen's Association (NAA) in 1938. Headquartered in Chicago, Brown became the spokesperson for the organization. Her personal determination and dedication helped win support for black participation in the CPTP.

Sometimes the NAA created "media events" to help call attention to the problems blacks were facing. For example, in the spring of 1939, Dale L. White and Chauncey E. Spencer, members of the NAA, decided to fly from Chicago to Washington, D.C., to prove to the nation that blacks had the ability to fly. Encouraged by U.S. Representative Everett Dirksen of Illinois and Dwight Green (who went on to become governor of state) but forced to use their own money, White and Spencer borrowed one thousand dollars from a Chicago racketeer to rent an ancient Lincoln-Paige biplane.

They were given a grand send-off from Harlem Field by the NAA, but a few hours later they were forced to land outside Sherwood, Ohio. With another loan from Robert L. Vann, publisher of the *Pittsburgh Courier*, the duo was able to get to Washington. Edgar Brown, a contact Vann had given them, introduced White and Spencer to Senator Harry S Truman from Missouri, who said, "If you guys had the guts to fly this thing to Washington, I've got guts enough to see that you get what you are asking!"

Dr. Robert Rose, author of *Lonely Eagles*, believed that Truman was "the man who probably did more to turn the tide toward the future of blacks in aviation than any other man or incident up to that time." Truman and other sympathetic political leaders pushed for congressional action inside the Senate to secure a place for blacks in the CPTP.

Congressional supporters were able to get Public Law 18 passed in April 1939, which made possible the establishment of pilot training programs at six black colleges and at two private aviation schools admitting black applicants. Public Law 18 was not a complete success since it did not open the Army Air Corps to African-Americans.

SLOW PROGRESS IN THE MILITARY

IN 1940, AMERICANS were dancing the lindy to the swing sounds of the
Benny Goodman and Tommy Dorsey bands, reading about Batman and
his sidekick, Robin, and laughing at the antics of Bugs Bunny.
Meanwhile, Nazi aggression swept across Europe. France fell under the

The German Luftwaffe (air force) was known for its devastating bombing
attacks on land and sea targets. (LIBRARY OF CONGRESS)

heel of the advancing German forces, led by the devastating German Luftwaffe (air force). And Britain was in a battle for its survival. Slowly Americans were beginning to realize that Nazism was a threat to the whole world, and that U.S. involvement in the war was inevitable.

Roosevelt, running for an unprecedented third term as the Democratic nominee for president of the United States, was openly shifting away from his neutral position, because he felt he had the nation's support. He had been elected in 1932 at a time when the country was in the stranglehold of the Great Depression. The Roosevelt administration had instituted federal public works programs of the New Deal, which put thousands of unemployed people back to work, constructing or repairing buildings, bridges, dams, and roads. After contracting polio, Roosevelt was confined most of the time to a wheelchair. Yet he inspired the nation's confidence by speaking to them on weekly radio broadcasts known as fireside chats.

He often spoke about the "four freedoms": freedom of speech and expression, freedom of worship, freedom from want, and freedom from fear. To blacks, these were high-sounding words without heart or soul, for in the United States they had not realized all these "freedoms."

Even though Roosevelt's record on civil rights was better than that of any president before him (he appointed an impressive number of women and minorities to key positions in government), there were those African-Americans who felt the administration could do much more, especially with regard to the Army Air Corps, which still would not accept blacks. African-American leaders argued that since the president is the commander in chief of the armed services, Roosevelt had the constitutional power to order the army to accept blacks in the air division. Roosevelt knew how to read the pulse of the nation, and in his opinion the political climate was not right to make that decision.

But northern blacks, who were becoming more politically astute, knew the importance of their votes to the Democratic coalition, and they kept the pressure on. The most vocal person on the issue of blacks in the military was Robert Vann, a lifelong supporter of black aviation and editor of the *Pittsburgh Courier*. In a stinging 1940 editorial, Vann reminded the public that while blacks couldn't fly, repair, or build aircraft, they were nevertheless taxed to support the expansion of the Army Air Corps.

Black pilots' organizations, including the NAA, publicized discriminatory practices within the New Deal agencies, especially in the CPTP. Black leaders warned that the Democratic Party was taking blacks for granted because they had voted for Roosevelt overwhelmingly in two elections. To offset the attacks and disclosures, the 1940 Democratic platform stated that the party would "continue to strive for complete legislative safeguards against discrimination in government service and benefits, and in the national defense forces."

Roosevelt's Republican opponent, Wendell Willkie, tried to woo blacks back to the party of "the Great Emancipator," Abraham Lincoln, by pledging to end segregation in the armed services. Several black newspapers endorsed Willkie.

In late September 1940, President Roosevelt arranged a meeting with three African-American leaders and members of the army and navy. The black leaders emphasized three points: (1) equal opportunity for jobs in the defense industry, (2) impartial administration of the new draft law, and (3) an opportunity for qualified blacks to learn to fly in *desegregated units*.

Because the meeting was held at the direct request of President Roosevelt, black leaders were expecting a good-faith response by the military, but this turned out to be a false hope. A few days later, the War Department issued a policy directive stating that black men generally would be admitted into the armed forces in numbers equivalent to their percentage in the civilian population. Additionally, the military brass agreed to start an all-black flying unit within the Army Air Corps.

President Franklin D. Roosevelt, circa 1940–41. (LIBRARY OF CONGRESS)

The War Department statement clearly implied that these new policies had the agreement and consent of the black participants. This was untrue and it provoked a furor when the black press accused them of "selling out" by agreeing to a separate air unit within the Army Air Corps. Walter White of the NAACP immediately sent a letter to the president criticizing the decision. The president wrote a personal letter to the three men stating: "You may rest assured that further developments of policy will be forthcoming to insure that Negroes are given fair treatment on a non-discriminatory basis."

On the heels of this letter, Roosevelt made three smart political moves. First, Colonel Benjamin O. Davis, Sr., was promoted to brigadier general in the United States Army. He was the first black in the regular army to hold that rank. The black press applauded the promotion for being not just a token gesture but a long overdue appointment that was well earned and well deserved. However, it was pointed out that Davis was almost sixty-four years old, a year short of retirement.

Davis's son wrote years later: "Although the promotion was motivated primarily by the hope of winning black votes in the 1940 presidential election, my father richly deserved it for many years. . . . After confirmation by the Senate, [my father] was ordered to command the 4th Cavalry Brigade, composed of the 9th and 10th Cavalry regiments—all-black except for the officers, some of whom were white." According to one editorial, "It was a small step, but at least it was in the right direction."

When General Davis received his orders, he requested and obtained the

40

William H. Hastie (1), civilian aid to the secretary of war, with Undersecretary of War Patterson, April 1942. (LIBRARY OF CONGRESS)

reassignment of his son, who was by that time promoted to captain. Having served several years at Tuskegee, teaching in the ROTC program, Captain Davis was excited about the transfer to Fort Riley, Kansas.

Captain Davis didn't know it then, but in a few months he'd be back at Tuskegee, and he'd be happy about it.

Meanwhile, President Roosevelt made another smart political move when he suggested that Secretary of War Henry Lewis Stimson appoint a black civilian adviser.

Stimson had served in the administrations of several presidents beginning with his appointment as secretary of war under William Howard Taft from 1911 to 1913. Although Stimson was a lifelong Republican, Roosevelt, a Democrat, appointed him secretary of war in 1940 to strengthen bipartisan support for American intervention in the war.

Stimson complained in his diary: "The Negroes are taking advantage of this period just before [the] election to try to get everything they can in the way of recognition from the army." Reluctantly, Stimson appointed William H. Hastie, a graduate of Harvard Law School and dean of the Howard University Law School. Hastie's job was to help develop policies that would improve conditions for blacks in all branches of the military.

Finally, Roosevelt appointed Colonel Campbell C. Johnson, also an African-American, adviser to the director of selective service.

These appointments were helpful in winning over many disillusioned black voters. Roosevelt captured the White House for a third term, and the African-American switch from the Republican Party to the Democratic Party was almost complete.

IN DECEMBER 1940, the Army Air Corps submitted a plan for an "experiment," which would establish an all-black fighter squadron. The press release stated that the 99th Fighter Squadron would consist of between thirty-three and thirty-five pilots and 278 ground crew members. The officers, however, were still going to be white. *Crisis* magazine praised the establishment of the 99th Fighter Squadron as "a step in the right direction . . . but it is by no means the answer to the demand of colored people for full integration into all branches of the armed services of the nation."

Hastie was less tactful. He flatly refused to endorse the "experiment," saying it was a national disgrace that a program was needed to prove that black men could fly an airplane. In his opinion, the army was not only continuing its segregation policy but expanding it.

Hastie immediately followed up with an official report to the secretary of war, pointing out that blacks were not 10 percent of the total military as the agreed-upon drafting policy stated. He also argued that keeping the military segregated was demeaning and demoralizing. He posed the following question in an interview that was reprinted in black newspapers across the country: "How could a black man be expected to fight and defend a country that didn't respect his rights as a citizen?"

General George C. Marshall, the army chief of staff, responded to Hastie's report by defending the military. "Segregation is an established American custom. The educational level of Negroes is below that of whites; the Army must utilize its personnel according to their capabilities; and experiments within the Army in the solution of social problems are fraught with danger to efficiency, discipline, and morale."

Hastie fired back a stinging rebuttal, but it didn't seem to make a difference. For the most part, Stimson ignored his recommendations. Hastie turned to the black press, which reported on his efforts.

"Hastie was our watchdog," said a veteran who was at Howard University during this time. "If he hadn't been there [at the War Department] scrapping for us, we wouldn't have gotten what little we were given."

"There were some of us guys who differed with Hastie about the integration thing," remembered another veteran who was also in college in Atlanta. "We were all glad when news of the Tuskegee experiment broke in the papers. At least we black fellows would have a chance to fly. We were young; the politics of the matter didn't register just then. We—I—wanted to fly, even if it was in segregated units!"

The plan to develop an all-black flying unit proceeded, but it still met with disapproval down in the ranks, and there were a few immediate and long-range concerns voiced in a flurry of recommendations and complaints to Secretary Stimson. One of the issues raised had to do with officers. Since it was considered a slight for white officers to be placed over blacks, the War Department decided that "*volunteer* white noncommissioned officers" would be used as "inspectors, supervisors, and instructors for an indefinite period of time. . . . Negro officers, when qualified, would replace white officers in the squadrons and in administrative positions."

One memo raised the issue of mechanics. "If there are Negro pilots then there *must* be Negro mechanics to service the planes." One military officer estimated that it would take "ten years to train a line chief, three years to train a crew chief, and two years for a hangar chief." Still, the decision was made that initial training for the ground crew that would service the planes for black pilots should take place within a year at Chanute Field in Rantoul, Illinois. Young black men were trained as airplane mechanics, aircraft armorers, aircraft supply and technical clerks, instrument operators, and weather forecasters. Hastie continued to fight for the rights of black servicemen, refusing to back down, even when other black leaders chose to give in. He became even more vocal when it came time to choose where the black pilots would be trained.

When California, Texas, Illinois, Michigan, and Tuskegee, Alabama, were suggested as possible training sites, Hastie favored Los Angeles, because it had a long and proud history of blacks in aviation. Howard Gould, an offical of the Chicago Urban League, fought long and hard for the Illinois site. In defending Chicago, Gould wrote to Hastie, noting that "the Harlem Air Field is not and never has been a Jim Crow airport." He referred to the outstanding CPTP programs located at the Coffey School of Aeronautics, located in Chicago and managed by Willa Brown, and the Glenview School outside Chicago. They were the only two noncollege institutions to offer CPTP, and they had successfully trained hundreds of black pilots in the pilot's training program. Gould, along with Walter White of the NAACP, persuaded Hastie to shift his support to Chicago. But the army had the final say.

In spite of the support for Chicago, Tuskegee emerged as the prime training site for black pilots. Hastie was furious. Why the South? he asked.

The South was different then. In 1940, Alabama was a stronghold of racial intolerance. The average income of blacks was 60 percent less than that of whites and only 2 percent of Alabama's black citizens could

vote. Blacks were subject to the lawless acts of the Ku Klux Klan and other hate groups, who maimed and murdered men, women, and children. Very little, if anything, was done in most cases to stop the violence.

African-Americans were subjected to signs like these in public places all over the country. They were especially painful to African-American servicemen and their families.
(LIBRARY OF CONGRESS)

44

Hastie expressed his and the black community's outrage that the War Department would even consider putting an all-black base in the South.

Captain Benjamin O. Davis, Jr., had taught at Tuskegee for several years and knew the racial tensions that existed there. He wrote later: "The Air Corps well understood the political mine fields that stood in the way of the airfield's development: the attitude of the white citizens of Tuskegee; the attitude of the white officers and enlisted men assigned to the base; the War Department's segregation policies; and the basic question posed by the . . . [Tuskegee] 'experiment.'"

Once again, over Hastie's and other black leaders' strong objections—almost in spite of them—Tuskegee was selected.

It is interesting to note that after the war, even General Marshall admitted to his biographer, "I might say here that one of the greatest mistakes I made during the war was to insist the colored divisions be trained in the South."

TUSKEGEE IS CHOSEN

THE SELECTION OF Tuskegee remains controversial even today. A few historians concluded, and with some documentation, that the army hoped—even expected—the program would fail. Others believe Tuskegee was chosen because it was the home of a famous black institution that stood for self-help and self-determination.

Not all black leaders agreed with Hastie's objection to placing the base in the South. More than a few African-Americans, especially black southerners, felt it was appropriate that the training of the all-black 99th Fighter Squadron should be near the institution built by Booker T. Washington, the former slave who had become one of the most prominent and respected leaders in America before his death in 1915.

Booker T. Washington, first president of Tuskegee Institute (later University) in Alabama. (LIBRARY OF CONGRESS)

Booker T. Washington's story, which he chronicled in his autobiography, *Up From Slavery*, has all the elements of a drama. After completing his education at Hampton Institute in Virginia, and teaching adult education classes there, Booker T. Washington was invited in 1881 by the citizens of Tuskegee to head a school for former slaves and their children.

Located about thirty miles from Montgomery, in central Alabama, Tuskegee grew out of the determination and drive of Washington and the people he hired to help him strive for excellence. Applying his basic philosophy of self-help, Washington turned a leaky barn into a model industrial arts school.

There is no doubt in anybody's mind that Washington was a fine educator. However, his involvement in the murky nineteenth-century political arena has become a source of controversy.

In 1895, a few months after the death of Frederick Douglass, Washington made his famous "Atlanta Compromise" speech at the Cotton Exposition. Washington accepted segregation as a "necessary condition for economic cooperation be-

Frederick Douglass was a prominent African-American leader who died the same year Booker T. Washington made his famous speech at the Atlanta Cotton Exposition, which catapulted Washington into a position of national leadership. (LIBRARY OF CONGRESS)

tween the races." He also suggested that the races could be as "separate as the fingers of the hand" in all things racial, "but one as the fist" in matters of national interest—such as war.

White leaders instantly declared Washington "the" spokesman for all African-Americans, without regard for those who disagreed with Washington's finger-fist analogy. W. E. B. Du Bois, one of the founders of the NAACP, disagreed with Washington, favoring integration. The debate over the two positions continues among African-Americans, but it is undeniable that during his lifetime, Booker T. Washington was a man who inspired people to do their best, to make the most out of what they had, and to strive to improve themselves. That philosophy became synonymous with Tuskegee, and for that reason some people believe it was chosen as the site for the Tuskegee "experiment."

Dr. Frederick Douglass Patterson, the third president of Tuskegee, and G. L. Washington, director of pilot training programs there, were strong supporters of black aviation. Patterson helped persuade Charles "Chief" Anderson to come to Tuskegee to head the school's CPTP.

Tuskegee had been late in securing CPTP certification because it didn't have a suitable airfield within the required "ten miles of the contracting institution." Patterson and Washington, along with local and state politicians, worked together to arrange for Tuskegee CPTP trainees to use a white airstrip until one could be built.

To get the financial backing he needed to complete the job, President Patterson invited the Rosenwald Fund of Chicago to hold its board meeting at Tuskegee. First Lady Eleanor Roosevelt, who was on the board of the foundation at the time, arrived early. She was shown the campus and given its history. Mrs. Roosevelt was very impressed.

After the informational meeting, Mrs. Roosevelt met "Chief" Anderson and his all-black crew of instructors. "Chief" Anderson remembered the conversation that day during an interview with television producer Tony Brown. "'Some say Negroes can't fly airplanes,' said

First Lady Eleanor Roosevelt was a strong supporter of African-American aviators. She took this plane ride with "Chief" Anderson at Tuskegee against the advice of her secret-service bodyguards. (NATIONAL AIR AND SPACE MUSEUM/SMITHSONIAN INSTITUTION)

Mrs. Roosevelt, smiling, 'but you seem to be flying around very well.'" Then the first lady requested that she be allowed to go up for a flight with "Chief" Anderson.

The secret service tried to discourage the first lady and even threatened to call the president, but Mrs. Roosevelt had strapped herself in, and no one dared stop her. "I took [Mrs. Roosevelt] up and we flew around for a bit, then landed," said "Chief" Anderson. Someone snapped a picture of Mrs. Roosevelt and Anderson, and it appeared in newspapers all over the country. "That plane ride did more for black aviation than anything had before."

After her visit to Tuskegee, Mrs. Roosevelt became a steadfast supporter of that institution. The Rosenwald Fund loaned the college $175,000 to construct Moton Field, Tuskegee Institute's CPTP training field.

Three
1941

THE EXPERIMENT BEGINS

DURING THE FIRST half of 1941, black people increased their demands for better job opportunities in the defense industry. The NAACP staged a National Defense Day to protest against discrimination in government hiring. And in June of 1941, labor leader A. Philip Randolph called for one hundred thousand blacks to march on Washington to protest discrimination in the armed services and in the defense industry. To avoid a confrontation at a time when the nation was preparing for war, Roosevelt issued Executive Order 8802, which forbade racial discrimination in government hiring and training programs.

A. Philip Randolph, president of the Brotherhood of Sleeping Car Porters, fought for equality of opportunity for black workers in the defense industry.
(LIBRARY OF CONGRESS)

In part, 8802 stated:

> I do hereby reaffirm the policy of the United States that there shall be no discrimination in the employment of workers in the defense industries or government because of race, creed, color or national origin, and I do hereby declare that it is the duty of employees and of labor organizations in furtherance of said policy and of this order, to provide for the full and equitable participation of all workers in defense industries, without discrimination because of race, creed, color, or national origin.

As the battle over civil rights in America heated up, so did the war in Europe. Roosevelt called for aid to nations fighting Nazi Germany in the form of a lend-lease plan, which permitted him to "sell, transfer title to, exchange, lease, lend, or otherwise dispose of ships, tanks, planes, guns and ammunition or other supplies to England." The Germans suspected that American ships were carrying weapons, and our own military records support their suspicions. The Germans retaliated by sinking an American freighter, the *Robin Moore*, and later in the year, a German "wolf pack" (a name used for German submarines working together) attacked an American convoy four hundred miles south of Iceland.

The German wolf-pack tactic was devised to counter the convoy system. A number of submarines lay in wait for a convoy, or groups of ships, to pass. The first captain to spot a convoy sent out a message to the others, and they all closed in for the kill. Convoys usually had heavy losses, but a single ship, like the *Robin Moore*, didn't have a chance.

Roosevelt spoke to the nation about German attacks on ships in the Atlantic Ocean. Americans were outraged by the loss of American ships and lives. Still, antiwar sentiments ran high. But most Americans were convinced it was just a matter of time before the United States would be pushed or pulled into the war against Nazi aggression.

50

Meanwhile, the formation of the first black combat unit in Army Air Corps history had been officially announced at a press conference on January 16, 1941. According to the official report: "Concurrently, 35 black candidates would be chosen under the Civil Aeronautics Authority (CAA) from the Civilian Pilot Training Program (CPTP) established by Congress in 1939 to train civilians while they were going to college, and given 30 weeks of flight training under white instructors." In addition, funding was also approved for a twenty-two-week program designed to train 460 enlisted support personnel at the Air Corps Technical School at Chanute Field in Illinois, who upon completion of the two programs, would be moved to Tuskegee, where an airfield would be established.

Moses McKissack (top) and Calvin McKissack of McKissack and McKissack, Inc., of Nashville, Tennessee, general contractors and builders of Tuskegee Army Air Field. (AUTHORS' PRIVATE COLLECTION)

The government awarded the building of Tuskegee Army Air Field (TAAF) to a black architectural and construction company, McKissack and McKissack, Inc., of Nashville, Tennessee. It was the firm's responsibility to convert an abandoned grave site into an airfield, complete with hangars, repair shops, classrooms, laboratories, administration building, flight surgeon's offices, separate dormitories, dining halls, firehouse, infirmary, and of course, the runways. The airfield was built in less than six months and at a cost of 1.1 million dollars, one of the largest government contracts ever awarded a black-owned business.

When William Hastie heard that the base was

being constructed with segregated facilities, he personally confronted General George Brett, chief of the Army Air Corps, and demanded that all construction of TAAF stop until the plans were changed. General Brett, however, decided that Hastie's demands were unreasonable. "They were unreasonable times," said General Benjamin Davis, Sr., during a recent interview.

The first group of cadets had been inducted into the Army Air Corps during March 1941, before the base was officially opened (though unfinished) on July 19, 1941. Officiating at the dedication ceremonies was Major General Walter Weaver, commander of the Southeastern Army Air Forces Training Command. He addressed the cadets, saying: "The success of the venture depends upon you . . . you cannot be inoculated with the ability to fly."

Construction of TAAF continued throughout the summer and fall of 1941 as the cadets arrived. The base was segregated, controlled by white officers who maintained it the same way civilian society wanted it kept in the rural South. Everything was separate and enforced by law. The first black trainees who came to TAAF ate in separate mess halls, used separate latrines (bathrooms) and recreation facilities. No black officers belonged to the officers' club.

Off base the situation was worse. Except for Tuskegee Institute, there were very few places for a black person to eat a meal, to shop, or to enjoy good entertainment. There were no local hotels that accommodated blacks, and the schools were segregated. Housing presented the most pressing problem to blacks stationed at Tuskegee. "The cadets could be put up at the Institute [Tuskegee], and later in barracks," a cadet wrote later. "But officers, civilian instructors, and base employees had to fend for themselves."

All the commanding officers of Tuskegee were white. The first was Major James A. "Straight Arrow" Ellison.

Major Ellison was a "by-the-book" officer who gave no quarter and

Tuskegee Army Air Field (TAAF) was built to be a segregated base with separate facilities for whites and blacks. Post headquarters is where the commanding officers made decisions and carried out orders. (GEORGE MITCHELL PRIVATE COLLECTION, TOP; CHRIS NEWMAN PRIVATE COLLECTION, BOTTOM)

asked for none when it came to army regulations. In the official history of the base, Ellison is quoted as saying he wanted to "make a go" of the project, and that his ambition was "to fly across country with a Negro squadron and prove to the nation that it could happen." Author Stanley Sandler described Ellison as "a decent, sincere, blunt, old pilot who had apparently even opposed some of the segregation policies prevailing in surrounding Macon County."

George Spencer "Spanky" Roberts, one of the cadets in the first class at TAAF, remembered Commander Ellison. "He told us to look at the man on our right and on our left, because on graduation day, they would be washed out. We, of course, didn't believe it. We promised each other that we'd hang in there no matter what. In the end, only five of us made it."

THE FIRST CLASS

CONTRARY TO THE official report which stated there would be thirty-five pilot trainees, the first class began with twelve outstanding young black cadets and one officer trainee, a total of thirteen. Among them were a scholar-athlete, a graduate of Johnson Smith College, and a graduate of Northwestern University in Chicago. The men came from small towns and large cities. Several had participated in CPTP, and one even had his private pilot's license. By the end of the five-week primary training period, all but five had been washed out, a term used when a pilot candidate failed any part of his training. A person could be washed out for not following instructions, poor attitude, or failing a test. The pressure was intense, and the men were under a great deal of stress. None of them wanted to wash out, but they did. Good men did.

Five of the thirteen original cadets entered the final phase of their training in the fall of 1941. They were: Lemuel R. Curtis, a policeman

Major General George E. Stratemeyer with members of the first class of pilots at TAAF to be graduated at the advanced flying school. (L to R) Lt. George S. Roberts, Capt. Benjamin O. Davis, Jr., Lt. Charles DeBow, Lt. Lemuel R. Curtis, and Lt. Mac Ross. (United States Air Force/Library of Congress)

from Hartford, Connecticut, and a Howard University graduate; Charles DeBow, a Hampton Institute graduate in business administration and a CPTP pilot; Mac Ross, a native of Dayton, Ohio, and a graduate of West Virginia State College and a CPTP pilot; George Spencer "Spanky" Roberts, a native of Fairmont, West Virginia, and a graduate of West Virginia State College; and Captain Benjamin O. Davis, Jr.

Captain Davis had been at Fort Riley only two weeks when he was told to report for a flight physical. He was going back to Tuskegee, but under vastly different circumstances. Instead of teaching military science, he was going to be participating in the newly formed 99th Fighter Squadron the army was starting.

When the flight surgeon learned that Davis was applying for the Army Air Corps, the doctors wrote down that Davis had epilepsy. In his autobiography, Davis concluded, "The failure of a good many other black pilot training applicants to qualify must have been based on similar policy directives to examining flight surgeons, who manufactured phony deficiencies." The records were "corrected" as mysteriously as they had been falsified, and Davis reported to TAAF, where he, along with the four other trainees, had reached the final stages of their training.

Running concurrently with the pilot training at TAAF was the Chanute Field Technical School for the training of aviation support personnel. The standards for admission were similar to those for the pilots, so many of the applicants came from African-American universities.

McGary Edwards, from West Virginia, was a student at Tuskegee Institute, majoring in mechanical engineering, when he heard about the program at Chanute Field. He applied and was accepted after passing rigid physical, psychological, and academic tests. "It was quite amazing to me to see the caliber of men being selected for induction [as auxiliary personnel]," said Edwards. "It must be remembered that none of these men were being selected for pilot training, yet their educational level, achievement in exam scores, and general qualifications should have rendered them all as officer candidates."

Once the trainees arrived at Chanute, they found the program poorly organized and confusing to everyone involved. Since the War Department wasn't sure about what role African-Americans were going to play in the military, there was a great deal of confusion regarding their training. But the message came down to Chanute that the training was to be taken seriously. Things changed. The 99th's support personnel were sent to Maxwell Air Force Base in Montgomery until early fall 1941, when the first five cadets were ready to fly. That's when the ground crew from Chanute arrived at TAAF.

Although a number of the flight instructors at TAAF were white southerners, they were by most accounts fair-minded. According to author Robert Rose, "The greater majority of cadets felt that the instructors were conscientious, having volunteered for duty at Tuskegee, insuring a degree of sincerity and fairness toward the students."

Those who were directly responsible for the training of the cadets of the 99th were: Captain Gabe C. Hawkins, the director of basic training who had been hurt in a crash but remained in the service as a non-flying officer; Captain Robert M. Long, known as Mother, was the director of advanced training; and Major Donald G. McPherson, who

was called Black Barney because even after shaving he had a twenty-four-hour five-o'clock shadow. Although these instructors were tough and often cantankerous, the cadets later appreciated their skill and experience.

Their first trainer plane was a PT-17, a biplane with unretractable landing gear. The instructor rode with the cadet during the first practice sessions, whether the trainee knew how to fly or not. The instructor worked the controls and demon-

TAAF trainees were given courses in math, map reading, communications, and other disciplines they would need to be good pilots. Sgt. George Mitchell was a communications instructor at the TAAF's Cadet Ground School from 1943 to 1946. (George T. Mitchell private collection)

strated different moves. The cadet was expected to follow the instructor's commands to the letter. Nothing would get a cadet washed out quicker than not following orders.

In case of engine failure, the pilot had to be aware of his options. If the nose went too high, or if the airspeed dropped too low, the plane would crash. The instructor set up several emergency situations and sometimes deliberately stalled the plane to see how the pilot would react under stress. After a number of flight hours with the instructor, the cadet was allowed to take the plane up solo.

The cadets then moved to advanced training in BT-13s, big "lumbering" airplanes. Each cadet gained confidence as he mastered stalls, practice landings, forced landings, spins, inverted flight, loops, slow rolls, snap rolls, vertical reverses, and other maneuvers that were required. Captain Davis's favorite was the chandelles, which were "abrupt, steep, climbing turns that had to be smoothly executed to gain maximum altitude and change of direction at the expense of airspeed. It is a beautiful and satisfying maneuver, requiring precision flying."

Next the cadets trained on the AT-6s, which had landing flaps, retractable landing gear, and a 650-horsepower engine. "In the AT-6," said Davis, "we fine-tuned the maneuvers we had learned in basic." Finally, as rated pilots the cadets were allowed to fly the P-40 fighter plane that was to be the main equipment of the 99th.

For Captain Davis, earning his wings was the completion of a dream that had begun when he was

Benjamin O. Davis, Jr. (National Air and Space Museum/Smithsonian Institution)

58

The airplanes that were used to train pilots at TAAF: (top to bottom) PT-17, BT-13, AT-6, P-40. (Maxwell Air Force Base Archives)

a child and his father had taken him to an air show. While Davis was at Tuskegee, "Chief" Anderson had taken Captain Davis up on a flight, but now he was actually flying his own aircraft. In his own words, flying was "a complete, unadulterated joy!"

Each time Davis slid into the cockpit of a plane, he felt a surge of excitement that never diminished throughout his career. "Flying over the green trees, the streams, and the orderly plots of farmland below was more exhilarating than anything I could have imagined."

Most of the men felt that way about flying even though every now and again, an irate farmer would take a shot at a low-flying airplane. Their love of flying helped them to endure the hardships of being away from home and loved ones—many of them for the first time.

Although the cadets were successful, there was always the underlying reminder that they were an *experiment*. "We weren't just men learning how to fly complicated machines," remembered a Tuskegee pilot. "Every time we climbed into a plane, we were carrying the weight of the entire black race on our backs. If we crashed, the race went down with us." The records show, however, that Tuskegee had a very low crash rate, possibly because the men were extra careful not to make mistakes. But crashes did happen. Lieutenant Mac Ross went on record for being the first airman to survive the loss of a military airplane, which made him a charter member of Tuskegee's "Caterpillar Club."

At about six thousand feet smoke started coming from his plane. Ross remained calm and kept his craft under control, but it was losing altitude fast. It looked as if he was going to ride it to the ground, but after much coaxing from his comrades, Ross finally bailed out and saved his life. When the aircraft crashed, Ross was heartsick. "I've wrecked a ship worth thousands of dollars," he thought, not thinking about his own narrow escape. "Maybe they'll think we're incompetent." Among the pilots, however, there was only one unpardonable sin, and that was to wreck an aircraft *on the ground*.

As the pilots neared the end of their training, the Japanese attacked Pearl Harbor in Hawaii, on December 7, 1941. This preemptive strike led the United States to enter World War II, fighting on two fronts—one in Europe and the other in the Pacific. The black cadets at TAAF had proved that black men could fly. Now the question was, Were they brave enough to fight?

Four 1942

SLOW PROGRESS AT TAAF

ONE THING WAS sure, the 99th Fighter Squadron was ready. The first class, 42-C, earned their wings in formal ceremonies on March 7, 1942. Meanwhile, Classes 42-D and 42-E were being trained and were graduated in five-week intervals.

After the United States entered the war, black men applied for admission to the Army Air Corps in larger numbers than the Army had expected. At first, the army held Tuskegee to rigid quotas, refusing to train more than ten students in each class, which meant a lot of good men were disqualified or just not considered. Others had to wait months before being called up.

George Haley had dropped out of Syracuse University in the fall of 1942 and rushed to join the Army Air Corps. Although he'd passed the pilot training test, he had to wait a year before he was called to report to Tuskegee.

It wasn't much different for Herman "Ace" Larson. He was a CPTP-trained pilot from Fresno State College and the only black in a class of twenty whites. When his friends all said they were going to sign up for the air force, Larson decided to go along, too. Larson was confronted by a major who yelled at him, "Get the hell out of here, boy, the army isn't training night fighters!"

Larson was angry and hurt, but he was determined to get in the air force. When he heard about Tuskegee, he wrote to his congressman, senator, and even President Roosevelt. He waited about nine months before getting word that he'd been accepted for aviation cadet training at Tuskegee.

At the time he was working as a photographer. He had about one thousand dollars worth of camera equipment in his 1935 convertible. Fearful that the army might change its mind, Larson drove straight to the train station, leaving his car there. He never saw his car or his camera equipment again.

Another problem arose when black youths mistakenly enrolled in the Tuskegee Institute CPTP, believing that it would automatically qualify them for further training in the Army Air Corps program at the Tuskegee Army Air Field (TAAF). Capitalizing on the problem, the president of Tuskegee Institute requested that the War Department qualify the school's field (Moton Field) as a primary training center for prospective cadets. The War Department readily approved the request.

After the first few classes graduated from TAAF, the army changed its procedure. The cadets still had to pass rigid physical and written examinations, but the cadets were given primary training at Moton Field under the supervision of "Chief" Anderson and his crew. (This was not an uncommon practice. All over the country, flying schools that were

Charles "Chief" Anderson. (NATIONAL AIR AND SPACE MUSEUM/SMITHSONIAN INSTITUTION)

close to air bases, like Moton Field, operated under contract with the Army Air Corps to give primary training to prospective cadets.)

Once the cadets passed the first part of their training at Moton, they were moved to TAAF, where they were given basic and advanced training. A majority of the Tuskegee Airmen who were trained at TAAF took their primary training at Moton Field under "the Chief."

The success of the first few classes helped ease some of the pressure regarding black abilities. But just as William Hastie had warned, the segregated facilities at TAAF and the local residents' attitudes toward black servicemen soon erupted into confrontations.

Captain Davis, who had endured four years of isolation at West Point, tried to convince his comrades that the best way to defeat racism was by being so good nobody could deny them the respect they deserved.

"We didn't want people to love us or to give us any special privileges," said Lieutenant Charles DeBow, one of the original five graduates of TAAF. "We wanted to be respected for being first rate pilots in the Army Air Corps. Nothing more. Nothing less."

One night members of the 99th flew an advanced training gunnery and mock bombing mission to Dale Mabry Field in Tallahassee, Florida. The

Colonel Frederick von Kimble (above) followed Maj. James Ellison as commanding officer of TAAF. (MAXWELL AIR FORCE BASE ARCHIVES)

pilots were tired when they arrived, but they had to sleep in the brig (jail) because they weren't allowed to sleep in the same barracks with white officers.

By spring of 1942, Colonel Ellison had been replaced by Colonel Frederick von Kimble, the new commander of TAAF. A West Point graduate with twenty-four years of flying experience, von Kimble alleged that Ellison had fallen out of favor with the local authorities when he defended a black security guard who had challenged a white civilian. Von Kimble rigidly enforced segregation on the base and posted "Colored" and "White" signs to make sure there were no mistakes about the army's position.

Von Kimble was from Oregon, but he embraced the customs of the Deep South with pleasure. It was noted by more than a few cadets that the commander was typical of a lot of northern whites who "bent over backwards to cater to what they perceived as the 'Southern way of life.'"

Von Kimble also set up "indoctrination" classes (segregated, of course) for northern whites and blacks who were coming to the South for the first time. The information in these classes excused segregation. Particularly offensive were the quotes from Booker T. Washington's finger-fist analogy from his 1895 Atlanta Compromise speech, which were used to suggest that segregation was "beneficial" to both blacks and whites. To all but a few, the orientation class was demoralizing.

In spite of everything, the goal to train black pilots, to develop mechanics, and to equip and organize a fighter squadron moved forward. Progress was made, albeit in unusual ways, as Captain Davis's promotion to lieutenant colonel shows.

Captain Davis was scheduled to be promoted to major, but on March 1, 1942, all the Army Air Force officers in the West Point class of 1936 were promoted to lieutenant colonel to fill the need for more wartime and well-trained officers. So Captain Davis became Lieutenant

Colonel Davis, skipping over the rank of major. Mrs. Davis named their new puppy Major to commemorate the event.

To fill the need for more and more recruits, the new 100th Fighter Squadron was activated on May 23, 1942. Lieutenant Mac Ross became the commanding officer. Lieutenant Colonel Benjamin O. Davis, Jr., took over the command of the 99th on August 24, 1942. Although Ross and Davis had taken over the command of these squadrons, white officers were still in command of the base.

TENSION EASES UNDER NEW COMMAND

ON DECEMBER 26, 1942, Colonel Noel F. Parrish replaced Von Kimble as commander of TAAF. He would remain there until after the war ended. Colonel von Kimble was transferred to Cockron Field in Macon, Georgia.

Years later, Parrish revealed that just before taking command of TAAF, General Weaver had told him "off the record" not to worry about standards or morale. "Keep 'em happy," he'd said. "Your job is just to keep 'em happy." Yet records show Weaver had been instrumental in getting the program started and even had written to Washington in defense of the program: "These Negroes are wonderfully educated and as smart as they can be, and politically they have behind them their race composed of some eleven million people in this country."

Clearly, mixed messages were being sent by the army to the field commanders. Parrish summarized the situation when he said, "At the time, no one in the U.S. Air Corps was pushing the idea of black participation, but no one could afford to be seen as opposing the idea either." An incident that happened to Lieutenant Colonel Davis supports Parrish's assertion regarding the high level of hypocrisy that surrounded the Tuskegee project.

In his autobiography, Davis described the events following a visit to the base in 1942 by Secretary of War Stimson.

Captain Benjamin O. Davis, Jr.'s photo (left rear) was spliced into this picture to make it appear as though Davis had met with Secretary of War Stimson, when, in fact, the two did not meet. (MAXWELL AIR FORCE BASE ARCHIVES)

Benjamin O. Davis, Sr. (l) and Jr. (r) with then Lt. Col. Noel Parrish (center), the third commanding officer of TAAF. Parrish, who later was made a general, stayed at TAAF until the war ended. (MAXWELL AIR FORCE BASE ARCHIVES)

The usual photographs of the occasion were taken, but when he returned to the Pentagon, someone asked for a photograph of him being greeted by me. I had not been asked to participate in the Secretary's visit in any way, and no such picture existed. Nevertheless, the word came down from Washington to furnish them with one. . . . I was called in to TAAF Headquarters and given a raincoat to put on, because it had been raining on the day of the Secretary's visit. They took my picture, superimposed it on a photograph that had actually been taken during the visit, and sent it to Washington. This phony photograph was mailed to the Pentagon to prove beyond a doubt that Lieutenant Colonel Davis had met Secretary Stimson at TAAF.

Under Colonel Parrish, Tuskegee became a different place—less restrictive, less depressing. Parrish, a native of Lexington, Kentucky, was born in 1909. After graduating from Rice University in Texas, he joined the army on July 30, 1930. By all accounts, he was a fine officer and the men respected him. "We didn't agree with him about a lot of things," recalled one of the former Tuskegee Airmen, "but he was so much better than the others, we sang satisfied."

Those who knew him said Colonel Parrish learned to despise segregation. "Segregation is discrimination," he was heard to say bluntly, and though he didn't have the authority to end segregation at TAAF, he did what he could to ease racial tensions. One of his first orders was to remove the "Colored" and "White" signs that had been so prominently placed on the base. By applying a little tact, a measure of humor, and sincere motives, he managed to keep the situation from exploding.

Parrish knew that the men were living in an isolated environment with very few amenities. He, with Dr. Frederick Douglass Patterson's help, brought in celebrities such as Lena Horne and Joe Louis to visit

African-American celebrities often visited TAAF. Here heavyweight boxing champion Joe Louis (r) is pictured with a member of the group. (NATIONAL AIR AND SPACE MUSEUM/SMITHSONIAN INSTITUTION)

the troops. Opera star Grace Moore and comedian Eddie "Rochester" Anderson gave shows that helped boost the men's spirits.

Sometimes Parrish was asked ridiculous questions, to which he had a ready answer. For example, when asked "How do Negroes fly?" Parrish would answer, "Oh, they fly very much like everyone else flies." But even Parrish was stunned by the ignorance of a local white who asked him, "Are those really Negroes up there or are you doing it for them?"

"No," Parrish answered and walked away, leaving the man to interpret the answer any way he chose.

68

The real test of Parrish's diplomacy and leadership came during an explosive incident, involving the airmen and Tuskegee citizens. One evening two white policemen confronted an airman, accused him of drunkenness, and tried to arrest him. He resisted. A black MP (Military Policeman), who happened to see the incident, knew that soldiers who were taken by the locals were often brutally beaten before being released. The MP drew his gun and forced the policemen to release the soldier to him. The whites were furious and mobbed them both, beat them, and put them in jail.

When word got back to the base that two TAAF men were in custody, two truckloads of black MPs and airmen armed themselves and took off for town. When Colonel Parrish heard about it, he headed them off and told the men to return to the base. Although they were full of resentment and anger, the soldiers obeyed their officer and returned to base, thus diverting a situation that could have erupted into a full-scale riot.

It is not known what Colonel Parrish said to the townspeople, but they weren't anxious to tangle with the United States Army—black or white. He secured the release of the two men and returned to the base. There was no battlefield in Tuskegee that night. Parrish revealed later, however, that the whites were in the process of passing out guns and ammunition they had bought and stored just in case there was a "black rebellion."

"We needed to vent our frustration," recalled a former Tuskegee pilot. "If we hadn't had each other, it would have been unbearable. How were we expected to hate Nazis for their atrocities, yet many of those same atrocities were taking place in the United States against us."

Most of the time the racial confrontations were not nearly so serious. Some were funny. In the film *Black Eagles*, Lieutenant Hannibal "White Folks" Cox, a pilot, told a story about how he used his fair complexion to make a mockery of color prejudice.

"Some of us went down to Elgin Air Force Base on a bus," Cox began his story. "My very, very close friend was Hugh White from St. Louis. . . . We were inseparable." Cox had fair skin. When the group got hungry, they stopped to get some sandwiches. They knew they couldn't go in the white restaurant, so White suggested that Cox go into the shop to buy food for them all. Cox went in and bought the sandwiches, pretending to be white. "When I got to the door of the bus," Cox said, laughing, "Hugh was at the door waiting for me. And just as I got ready to go in the door, Hugh hauled off and hit me upside the head and knocked me down the steps. As I got up, I said, 'Hugh, why did you hit me?' He said, 'Hannibal, you played the role just right, but you said *nigger* one too many times.'"

As 1942 came to a close, the men of the 99th and 100th wanted to know when they would be called into action. Nobody knew the answer. Rumors spread and tempers flared. Although the officers tried to assure the men that orders would be coming soon, even they weren't sure about what was going on. Nobody knew. But Davis took comfort in knowing that his pilots were ready for combat.

William Hastie, African-American newspapers, and the NAACP continued to apply pressure, demanding answers regarding the fate of the Tuskegee Airmen. Were these well-trained men going to be put in mothballs before they ever got a chance to complete the "experiment"?

70

Five 1943

THE 99TH IN ACTION

THE WAR DEPARTMENT didn't know what to do with the black pilots it had trained. The Tuskegee plan hadn't been expected to succeed nearly so well; no real consideration had been given beyond their training. It was decided to move the men to "another location," so they would think some action was being taken. But where could the army send them? Three fighter squadrons usually make up a fighter group. The 99th Fighter Squadron didn't belong to a group; they were a fourth squadron. They became known as the Lonely Eagles.

Someone on Secretary of War Stimson's staff came up with the idea of sending the 99th to Liberia, in West Africa, which had been founded by former slaves who had returned to Africa. (Colonel Charles Young had served briefly as military attaché there prior to and after World War I.) According to military correspondence, in Liberia the squadron would be ordered to "search for German submarines preying upon convoys along the west coast of Africa." The plan was a cruel joke in military circles. The limited range of the fighter aircraft would have rendered the 99th ineffective and the mission meaningless.

It was over this issue, and the creation of a committee on special

71

Members of the 99th Fighter Squadron in North Africa. For the young black airmen, being on the continent of Africa was an eye-opening experience.
(NATIONAL AIR AND SPACE MUSEUM/SMITHSONIAN INSTITUTION)

troop policies known as the McCloy Committee, that Judge William Hastie resigned from the War Department, effective January 31, 1943. Stimson had asked his assistant, John J. McCloy, to organize the committee. It wasn't so much that Hastie objected to the committee itself, but he had not been involved in the formation of the group or invited to participate. In his opinion the McCloy Committee was a way of circumventing his authority, which was already limited. Truman K. Gibson, Jr., was appointed to fill Hastie's position.

After Hastie's much publicized resignation, the army reexamined its decision about where to use the 99th. The Allies needed tactical fighters in North Africa, which provided a perfect solution for the army. The 99th boarded ship on April 15, 1943, bound for North Africa.

Lieutenant Colonel Davis remembered that spring day in 1943, when the 99th left Tuskegee: "As we said our good-byes, we pushed far back and away the ugliness that we had endured. After all, we had successfully passed the first obstacle standing in the way of a better life for all of us—learning how to fly airplanes."

72

For over three years, British troops had been trying to stop the German and Italian forces from taking control of the Suez Canal. For a while, the enemy troops were the aggressors, capturing strategic points along North Africa's Mediterranean border. Field Marshal Erwin Rommel drove the British back into Egypt during June, 1942. Meanwhile, Adolf Hitler committed a large number of troops and supplies to the land war against Russia, which meant that he couldn't provide the support Rommel needed in Africa. Britain was supported by troops from New Zealand, Australia, and a special detachment of United States Air Force, long-range B-24 bombers. Using their united strength the Allies pounded enemy strongholds and Italian ships located in the Mediterranean Sea. On July 7, the tide turned in favor of the Allies when the British stopped the Germans at El Alamein, about 210 miles west of the Suez Canal.

Allied forces continued to inflict heavy losses on enemy armored units throughout the fall of 1942, and by November they had broken through Rommel's lines.

By the time the 99th arrived in Morocco on May 1, 1943, the Germans had been pinned against the sea and the battle for North Africa was essentially over.

When the ship pulled into harbor, the men of the 99th got their first glimpse of Africa. They were immediately surrounded by Arab youths, who begged them for cigarettes and food.

"We were in Africa, a place where having dark skin was the norm. It was the whites who looked out of place there," recalled one of the former 99th pilots in an interview. Most of the men had never been out of their home states except for their military training, and certainly none of them had seen the colorful robes of Berber traders astride magnificent horses or camels.

Their first camp was located at Oued N'ja (pronounced Wedenja) near Fez. According to Lieutenant Colonel Davis: "The town of Fez was found to be one of the most delightful spots that any of us had ever visited. . . . Our relations with the other troop units in the area were excellent, and it was easy to enjoy the free and open customs of this region and forget the hateful attitudes that dominated our lives in the United States."

Josephine Baker, the well-known African-American performer, who had become a French citizen, entertained the troops, but she insisted that the audience be integrated. Baker introduced black officers to prominent French and Moroccan families, which angered some white officers, who felt slighted.

Soon after their arrival, the squadron received its supply of P-40L War Hawks, a generation of the Curtiss-built fighter that could reach speeds of up to 350 miles per hour, climb over twenty-two-thousand feet, and ferry over one thousand miles. The pilots immediately got acquainted with their aircraft and tested themselves in flight drills and mock dogfights (combat between two fighter planes in close proximity). Much to their surprise, the men of the 99th were welcomed by members of the 27th Fighter Group, who chose to disregard the race taboos that might have kept them apart in the states. The pilots trained with each other several times.

The fliers of the 99th were particularly impressed with Colonel Philip Cochran, a famous American pilot who was the prototype for Flip Corkin, a comic strip character from the adventure series "Terry and the Pirates" by Milt Caniff. The few times Cochran trained with the 99th, the men learned a lot from him. "He imbued all of us with some of his own very remarkable fighting spirit," a pilot said, summarizing the special relationship the 99th had with Cochran.

After a month in Fez, the 99th was attached to the 33rd Fighter Group under the command of Colonel William "Spike" Momyer, located at Fardjouna, near Tunis. The former German airfield was littered with wrecked Me-109's (formerly known as BF-109s), considered by

74

many to be the best fighter in the war. Certainly it was one of the few times the men of the 99th would get a chance to see the enemy aircraft on the ground. Lieutenant Colonel Davis, who inspected one of the derelicts, was impressed with "its smallness and the efficiency of its cockpit design."

With North Africa secure in the hands of Allied forces, the generals decided that a group of Mediterranean islands, still controlled by Germany and Italy, needed to be captured to serve as stepping stones to the larger island of Sicily, which was the backdoor to Italy. The first target was Pantelleria. A few days after arriving in Fardjouna, Davis received orders that the 99th was to be sent on a mission.

BLACK EAGLES IN COMBAT

IN THE WORDS of its commander, Lieutenant Colonel Benjamin O. Davis, Jr., "No Army Air Force [AAF] unit had gone into combat better trained or better equipped than the 99th Fighter Squadron." But the men lacked actual combat experience.

Their first few missions were uneventful, mostly strafing—low-flying maneuvers used to destroy ground targets such as ammunition truck convoys, storage depots, and small farmhouses that were often used as field headquarters. They also flew bombing escort missions over the small island of Pantelleria. The bombers—B-17s and B-24s— were heavy and hard to maneuver, so they needed the protection of the smaller and faster fighters. During this phase of the war, escort pilots were ordered never to pursue an enemy and leave a bomber unprotected. If attacked, they were to hold position and fight off enemy aircraft without abandoning the bombers.

On the morning of June 9, 1943, members of the 99th were escorting a group of twelve bombers on a routine mission when they were

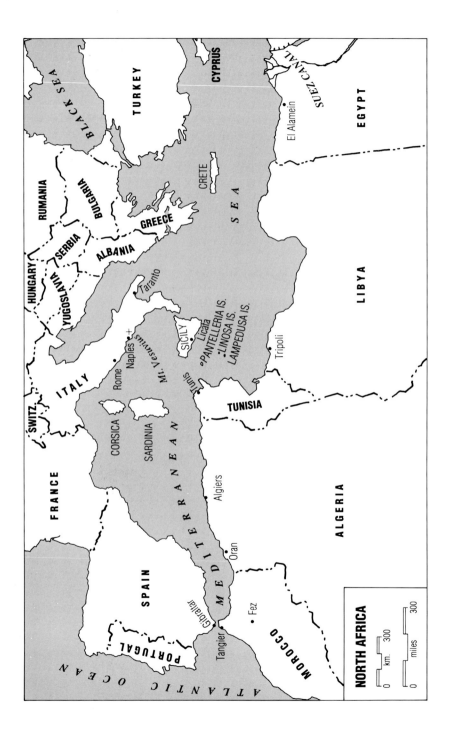

Captain Charles B. Hall, the first Tuskegee Airman to shoot down an enemy aircraft, on July 2, 1943. (NATIONAL AIR AND SPACE MUSEUM/SMITHSONIAN INSTITUTION)

attacked by four German Me-109s. Eight of the fighters stayed with the bombers and escorted them home, but four of the pilots broke off and pursued the enemy. These inexperienced pilots had broken rank by moving out of formation, a seemingly small infraction, but it almost cost the 99th its status as a battle-ready fighter squadron.

Throughout the rest of June and July the 99th participated in the bombing of Pantelleria. Then, on July 2 (although some references state July 21), Lieutenant Charles Hall scored the first kills for the 99th, when he downed a FW-190 and damaged an Me-109.

Later that day, General Dwight D. Eisenhower, who was at the time commander of American forces in North Africa, visited the squadron and praised Hall for an outstanding job. But the prize Charlie Hall cherished even more than the handshake of a general was the ice-cold cola his friends presented him.

The success of the victory was diminished by the deaths

General Dwight D. Eisenhower (rear), commander in chief of Allied forces during World War II. (LIBRARY OF CONGRESS)

Secretary of War Stimson (center) is pictured here with Lt. Col. Benjamin O. Davis, Jr. (l) and Lt. Gen. Carl Spaatz (r), commander of the Army Air Force in Northwest Africa. (LIBRARY OF CONGRESS)

of Lieutenants Sherman White and James McCullin, the first squadron casualties. Lieutenant Colonel Davis remembered the effect these and other deaths had on the men. "The loss of fighter pilots was like a loss in the family. On each combat mission, members of the squadron watched the takeoffs and were always on hand in large numbers to count the planes as they returned."

A few days later, when Pantelleria surrendered, the area commander, Colonel J. R. Hawkins, wrote to Lieutenant Colonel Davis:

> I wish to extend to you and the members of the squadron my heartiest congratulations for the splendid part you played in the Pantelleria show. You have met the challenge of the enemy and have come out of your initial christening into battle stronger qualified than ever. Your people have borne up well under battle conditions and there is every reason to believe that with more experience you will take your place in the battle line along with the best of them.

The 99th also participated in missions that resulted in the capture of two islands, Lampedusa and Linosa, which fell within days. This was the first time in history that air power alone had completely destroyed all enemy resistance. Following this success, the invasion of Sicily began in mid-July.

The rest of the summer the 99th made routine escort runs but scored no more kills. Then, quite unexpectedly, Lieutenant Colonel Davis was called back to the States to take command of the all-black 332nd Fighter Group (FG), which would consist of three all-black squadrons—the 100th, the 301st, and the 302nd—and a technical support group. Although the FG had been activated in 1942 at Tuskegee, the center for training had moved to Selfridge Field in Michigan, where conditions were less crowded.

BLACK EAGLES UNDER ATTACK

WHEN LIEUTENANT COLONEL Davis said good-bye to the 99th, he reminded his men that they were veterans of the Pantelleria and Sicilian campaigns and that this was something to be proud of. Davis left Europe, believing without a doubt that "the squadron would continue to develop and improve its performance."

Unfortunately, Colonel Momyer had other ideas. Momyer asserted in an *unofficial* written report that the black pilots lacked discipline and motivation in the air, and subtly placed into question the ability and courage of the 99th. Using the example of their *first* combat mission during which several of the pilots broke rank, he implied that their formations *frequently* disintegrated under fire. He wrote: "Their formation flying has been excellent until attacked by the enemy, when the squadron seems to disintegrate. On numerous instances when assigned to dive-bomb a specified target, though anti-aircraft fire was light or inaccurate, they chose a secondary target which was undefined. On one specified occasion, the 99th turned back before reaching the target because of the weather. The other [white] squadron went on to the tar-

The 99th's commanding officer, Col. B. O. Davis, says good-bye to his men at Licata, Sicily, August 1943, before returning to the United States to take command of the newly formed 332nd Fighter Group. (NATIONAL AIR AND SPACE MUSEUM/SMITHSONIAN INSTITUTION)

get and pressed home the attack." In summary, Momyer ranked their overall performance unsatisfactory:

> Based on the performance of the 99th Fighter Squadron to date,
> it is my opinion that they are not of the fighting caliber of any
> squadron in this group. They have failed to display the
> aggressiveness and daring for combat that are necessary to be
> a first class fighting organization. It may be expected that we will
> get less work and less operational time out of the 99th Fighter
> Squadron than any squadron in this group.

When Davis, who was back in the States, heard about the report, he was furious. Why hadn't Momyer confronted him with the problems

80

when they were first observed? By then the report was on its way up the military chain of command. Unbelievably, it was endorsed by officers who had just praised the pilots a few weeks earlier. General Edwin House, commanding officer of the 12th Air Support Command, fully endorsed the report and added, "The Negro type has not the proper reflexes to make a first-class pilot." The report was ushered through the chain of command all the way up to General Henry "Hap" Arnold, commanding general of the Army Air Force in Washington, D.C.

General Dwight D. Eisenhower was among those who did not agree with the report. In his opinion, the pilots of the 99th had performed admirably given their limited experience.

Ernie Pyle, a war correspondent who covered various phases of the Italian campaign, also helped to shed some light on why the 99th didn't have as many "kills" as other fighter squadrons. In his book *Brave Men*, Pyle described the action of the 99th: "Their job was to dive bomb, and not get caught in a fight. The 99th was very successful at this, and that's the way it should be."

Yet criticisms of the black airmen's combat performance had taken on a snowball effect. *Time* magazine had published an article in its September 20, 1943, issue, revealing plans that were being made to "disband the 99th as a fighter unit and attach the squadron to the Coastal Air Command, where it would be assigned routine convoy cover." Obviously, classified information about the squadron's future role in the Army Air Force had been leaked to the press, and on September 30, the *New York Daily News* further fanned the fires of misunderstanding by running a completely fabricated article by reporter John O'Connell stating that the 99th had been broken up and its members returned to the United States. The War Department immediately denied the article and assured the press that no plans were being made to deactivate the 99th or to discontinue training of the 332nd Fighter Group.

It was decided that Momyer's assessment of the 99th would be put before the Advisory Committee on Negro Troop Policies—the McCloy Committee. Lieutenant Colonel Davis was called to testify. Although he was outraged by the necessity for an inquiry, he realized the importance of getting the facts put in an "official" form. Davis answered the questions calmly and efficiently, supporting his statements with fact rather than conjecture. The committee called for a G-3 investigation, which ultimately revealed that the 99th "performed on a par with other P-40 Squadrons in the Mediterranean Theater of Operation."

Lieutenant Colonel Davis returned to Selfridge, where training of the 332nd Fighter Group continued.

THE LONELY EAGLES

MEANWHILE THE 99TH—the Lonely Eagles—had become the *fourth* squadron of the 79th Fighter Group (which was part of the 12th Air Force) on October 7, 1943, located at the Foggia Air Field complex in Italy. Colonel Earl E. Bates, the commanding officer, treated the 99th as an important part of the group and quietly and unobtrusively began integrating them into missions.

The 79th was a seasoned combat unit from whom the 99th, under the command of Major George "Spanky" Roberts, learned a great deal. "With this change came more experience and with the experience came confidence," said Roberts.

For example, Lieutenant Alva N. Temple gained the admiration and respect of everyone when during a takeoff his landing gear was damaged. He continued his mission, knowing that when he returned he would have to land without wheels. He did it and only lost part of his right wing.

By September, the Allies had captured Foggia and Sardinia; then Naples and Corsica collapsed in October. Field Marshal Albert

Kesselring had retreated from Sardinia to the Volturno River, but by late October his troops had fallen back to the Garigliano River. The 12th Air Force was ordered to keep the Germans retreating up the boot of Italy and to cut off their supplies and reinforcements.

EUROPEAN WAR THEATER-NOVEMBER, 1942

Dennis O'Brien

The 79th Fighter Group supported the ground troops by dive-bombing and strafing rail yards, supply convoys, highways, bridges, and depots. Throughout the summer and fall of 1943, black newspapers

83

back home reported how the 99th pilots were taking part in the Allies' victories in Italy.

The soldiers on the front were getting word from home that many of the cities in their homeland had turned into battlefields. Since May there had been a series of race riots. One in Mobile, Alabama, started when white employees objected to the promotion of twelve black workers in a defense plant. Black people were beaten and their homes and churches burned. While the 99th was strafing enemy positions in the Pantelleria campaign, there were riots in Detroit, Michigan; Beaumont, Texas; and Harlem in New York City.

The year ended on a bittersweet note for William Hastie, who had resigned from the War Department in January. The NAACP honored him with a Spingarn Medal for his "distinguished career as a jurist and as an uncompromising champion of equal rights." Hastie had fought for—and won—greater participation by blacks in the military. For example, in 1940 there were less than 5,000 blacks and only two officers above the rank of major among the 230,000 individuals in the army. By 1944, there were 702,000 blacks in the army, 165,000 in the navy, 17,000 in the marines, and 5,000 in the coast guard. The numbers jumped, in part, because of the war, but due to Hastie's ceaseless efforts, the conditions under which they served were somewhat improved.

In his acceptance speech, Hastie, who would become a distinguished judge, reminded the audience that African-Americans were in a war against oppression in their own country, and said that until the nation lived up to its promise of democracy, there could never be an "honest peace."

SIX
1944

THE 332ND

A FEW DAYS after the Allied Forces landed in Anzio in January 1944, the three squadrons of the 332nd Fighter Group arrived at Taranto, Italy. They were attached to the 62nd Fighter Wing, 12th Air Force. Lieutenant Colonel Benjamin O. Davis, Jr., their commanding officer, was upset when he learned the 332nd was assigned to coastal patrols in

Members of the 332nd being briefed. (NATIONAL AIR AND SPACE MUSEUM/SMITHSONIAN INSTITUTION)

obsolete P-39Q Airacobras, which in the words of one frustrated pilot "just didn't have enough to close in on the enemy." Lieutenant Colonel Davis believed the army's decision to place the 332nd in a noncombat role was a betrayal of everything he and his men had worked to achieve.

During the spring, Mount Vesuvius erupted and spewed volcanic ash for miles. The men had to wear gas masks and eye masks because of the fine dust that covered everything. Meanwhile, Lieutenant Colonel Davis learned that he had been awarded the Legion of Merit for his service with the 99th, and in May he was promoted to full colonel.

Within days Colonel Davis and the 332nd were transferred to the 306th Wing, 15th Fighter Command as bomber escorts and would be given P-47s to complete the mission. "Needless to say, I leaped at the opportunity," wrote Davis. "The escort mission was vitally important to the war, and our new aircraft would enable us to meet the Germans with the same altitude and speed capability."

The Republic P-47 Thunderbolt, known as "the Jug," was a tight machine with an overall length of thirty-six feet one and three-six-teenths inches. The P-47's auxiliary fuel tank permitted pilots to escort bombers longer distances, yet it was a sturdy fighter that could take a hit and still keep flying.

The black pilots welcomed their new fighters and respected the aircraft's ability, but they weren't intimidated by its advanced design. Several representatives from Republic Aircraft Manufacturers were sent to teach the 332nd how to fly the P-47. Staff Sergeant Samuel Jacobs remembered the visitors' surprise when they learned the black pilots had made the transition without them.

> I remember this Major standing atop a munitions carrier telling us "boys" all about the *flying bathtub* and how it should never be slow rolled below a thousand feet, due to its excessive weight. No sooner had he finished his statement than "A" flight was

> returning from its victorious mission. Down on the deck, props
> cutting grass, came Lieutenants [Wendell] Pruitt and his wingman Lee
> Archer, nearly touching wings. Lieutenant Pruitt pulled up into the
> prettiest victory roll you'd ever see, with Archer right in his
> pocket, as the Major screamed, "You can't do that!"

Pruitt's slow roll was risky, but he was young, spirited, gutsy, and a very good pilot. So were most of the men of the 332nd. Colonel Davis was proud of their ability, too, but he maintained a tough, no-nonsense position when it came to discipline. He did not approve of hotdogging and often fined pilots or sometimes even grounded them for showing off or taking unnecessary chances.

Most of the men had nicknames, even Colonel Davis. Usually he was referred to as Skipper or B. O., his initials. Roy Acuff, a popular country and western musician, had recorded a hit song about a man who was stern and proper but a very good teacher. Acuff called his teacher the Speckled Bird. So Davis's men adopted that name for their commanding officer. "But, none of us ever dared to call him that to his face," remembered a former pilot.

The men painted the tails of their P-47 aircraft red, so they became known as the Red Tails. World War II pilots and their crews also personalized their aircraft with slogans, nicknames, mes-

Lieutenant (later Capt.) Wendell Pruitt, of St. Louis, Missouri, described as a quiet and unassuming man on the ground, was a gutsy and topnotch pilot in the air. (MAXWELL AIR FORCE BASE ARCHIVES)

Lieutenant. Chris Newman (1) pilot of the <u>Goodwiggle</u>. Newman survived two crashes. (CHRIS NEWMAN PRIVATE COLLECTION)

The pilots depended on the skills of the ground crews who helped keep their aircraft operational and ready for combat. Here John T. Fields, an armament technician, loads a P-51 with ammunition. (CHRIS NEWMAN PRIVATE COLLECTION)

When the pilots weren't flying missions, they tried to relax. B. O. Davis, Jr., enjoys a challenging game of chess. (LIBRARY OF CONGRESS, PRINTS AND PHOTOGRAPHS DIVISION, TONI FRISSELL COLLECTION

sages, puns, designs, but more often their wife's or girlfriend's name. The black pilots had their traditions, too. Some of the names and messages painted on the Tuskegee Airmen's planes came from popular African-American songs, slang, and movies, such as *The Good Wiggle, Money Honey, Harlem Speaks, Pretty Lady,* and *Sweetie Pie.* The beautiful actress Lena Horne was their pinup girl, but the soldiers loved to show off their own women who were waiting for them back home.

Aside from camp routine, the men organized a theater group and gave a series of one-act plays. The 100th even had its own newspaper. There was a squadron chorus and a series of basketball, softball, and chess tournaments. They pieced together a makeshift "officers' club," called "the Panther Room," where they came to play cards and swap tales.

Back in February, General Eisenhower, who by that time was commander of the Supreme Headquarters of the Allied Expeditionary Force—known as SHAEF—had issued the following orders: "You will enter the continent of Europe and, in conjunction with the other united nations, undertake operations aimed at the heart of Germany and the destruction of her armed forces." Now the 332nd was going to be part of that undertaking.

By late May, nearly three million Allied soldiers, sailors, and airmen were standing ready for the invasion of Normandy, known as D-Day.

89

Although German intelligence knew that a massive invasion was going to take place, they didn't know when and where.

Eisenhower and his staff decided that based on the tides, the best days to launch D-Day were June 5, 6, or 7. Then they waited for the weather to make the final decision. On Sunday, June 4, a gale blew up, but forecasts suggested that Tuesday would be mild, followed by more bad weather on Wednesday. Eisenhower chose to move during the tiny window open on Tuesday morning, June 6, 1944. At 3:32 A.M., New York time, D-Day began. Thousands of soldiers swarmed the beachheads at Utah, Omaha, Gold, Juno, and Sword. (These were code names given by the military for five French beaches.)

Hitler was fast asleep at his headquarters during the invasion, doped with barbiturates, and no one was willing to wake him. When two of Hitler's generals warned him that the situation was critical, the führer told them to hold their positions at all costs. Clearly Hitler was mad.

The 332nd flew missions along with the 306th Fighter Group on June 7, and so did the 99th, which was still attached to the 79th Fighter Group.

Luftwaffe pilots were ordered by the German air command to concentrate their attack on Allied bombers. General "Hap" Arnold changed his policy and ordered U.S. fighters "to take the offensive, rather than to provide position defense to friendly bombers." That

Hitler and Mussolini, leaders of the Axis Powers. (LIBRARY OF CONGRESS)

90

meant escort pilots could break rank and pursue enemy fighters instead of staying strictly with the bombers. This is exactly what the 99th had been criticized for doing on its first mission.

With the freedom to pursue and destroy enemy fighters now, the 332nd's victories mounted quickly. On June 9, the Red Tails scored five victories in one day. Lieutenant Wendell Pruitt of the 302nd was credited with the first kill. In his own words he described what happened.

> We were assigned to fly top cover for heavy bombers.
> On approaching the Udine area, a flock of Me-109s were observed making attacks from 5 o'clock on a formation of B-24s. Each enemy aircraft made a pass at the bombers and fell into a left rolling turn. I rolled over, shoved everything forward and closed in on a 109 at about 475 mph. I waited as he shallowed out of a turn, gave him a couple of two second bursts, and watched him explode.

Wendell Pruitt of the 302nd Fighter Squadron with a crew chief, working on his aircraft to make sure it is combat ready. (CHRIS NEWMAN PRIVATE COLLECTION)

As the experience of the pilots of the 332nd grew, so did their confidence. On June 25, 1944, two pilots of the 302nd Fighter Squadron sank a German warship (destroyer) in the Adriatic Sea, the first time such a feat had been accomplished by fighter aircraft in the history of the Army Air Corps. The three-hour-and-fifteen-minute mission began when Lieutenants Larry Wilkins, Wendell Pruitt, Freddie Hutchins, and Gwynne Peirson were selected to be part of a four-plane, low-level attack on ground troops in Yugoslavia. Their orders were to fly the entire mission at a low altitude (fifty feet) and to make no radio contact.

Before reaching their target, Hutchins was hit by ground fire. He had to turn back. Larry Wilkins stayed with him. Meanwhile Pruitt and Peirson continued the mission. They never made contact with the enemy troops, but as they turned to recross the Adriatic Sea on their way back to the base, Pruitt and Peirson spotted a German destroyer in the Gulf of Trieste on its way out into the Adriatic.

Maintaining radio silence and flying at a dangerously low level, the two pilots decided to try the impossible. They made a run on the destroyer with their guns blasting. "After the first few bursts," wrote Peirson, "the next burst struck at the ship's waterline and started to 'walk' up its side." Then the ship exploded.

The 15th Air Force was skeptical upon hearing that two fighters had sunk a destroyer, but wing cameras on Peirson's P-47 provided the proof that by accurately placing machine gun fire they had accomplished what no other fighter group could boast.

In late June the three squadrons of the 332nd were transferred to Ramitelli Air Field on the east coast of Italy and attached to the 15th Air Force. At the time, the 99th was the lonely fourth squadron attached to the 79th Fighter Group. Now they were being transferred to Ramitelli and made a fourth squadron of the 332nd.

By that time, the pilots of the 99th had flown more than 298 missions in the Italian theater and a total of 3,277 sorties, missions in

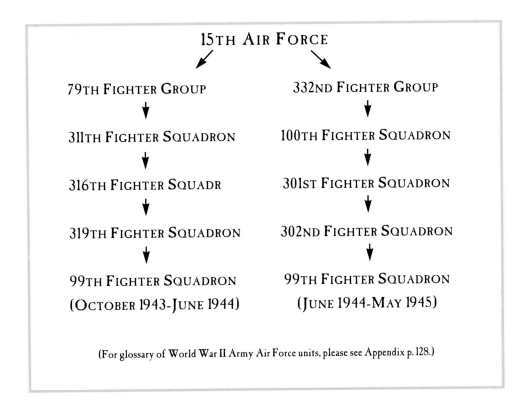

15TH AIR FORCE

79TH FIGHTER GROUP   332ND FIGHTER GROUP

311TH FIGHTER SQUADRON   100TH FIGHTER SQUADRON

316TH FIGHTER SQUADR   301ST FIGHTER SQUADRON

319TH FIGHTER SQUADRON   302ND FIGHTER SQUADRON

99TH FIGHTER SQUADRON   99TH FIGHTER SQUADRON
(OCTOBER 1943–JUNE 1944)   (JUNE 1944–MAY 1945)

(For glossary of World War II Army Air Force units, please see Appendix p. 128.)

which they encountered the enemy. They were frustrated and angry about their transfer because they feared losing "their identity." They had fought in an integrated group and held their own. They also saw their transfer to the all-black 332nd as the AAF's retreat from integration. If they were going to be a "fourth" squadron in a fighter group, the 99th wanted to stay with the 79th Fighter Group. Having been a part of the original 99th, Colonel Davis explained why its members took pride in their uniqueness: "The 99th was an isolated squadron, the first black flying unit, and not affiliated with any fighter group. . . . All its people were deeply aware of the necessity to demonstrate their ability in ways that would reflect favorably upon their proud unit."

Captain Vance Marchbank, flight surgeon of the 332nd, temporarily grounded a few of the 99th's pilots because they were suffering from battle fatigue and stress. To help alleviate flight stress and to assist the

99th in adjusting to the move, Captain Marchbank established Saturday-night talk sessions. Pilots were invited to discuss their anger, concerns, and fears.

There was some resentment at first among the men of the 99th and 332nd, but these talks helped to relieve many of the frustrations and tensions that had mounted over the months of duty. And as soon as the men began flying missions together, they became a cohesive unit, especially when they were assigned their new P-51 Mustangs, coveted by most pilots because of their speed.

The 99th was transferring from P-40s, while the 332nd was moving out of P-47s, which its pilots had been flying for only about a month. The P-51 fighters would remain the aircraft of the 332nd—including the 99th—for the duration of the war, recognizable by the familiar red markings on the tails. The squadrons within the 332nd had further distinguishing identifications. The trim tags of the 99th were white, the 100th black, the 301st blue, and the 302nd yellow. All fighters in the group had red spinners and red wing bands. Again the 99th was somewhat different; its bands did not extend to the wing tips as did those of the other three squadrons in the 332nd.

Meanwhile there was an anti-Hitler plot brewing in Germany. The German generals could see that the outcome of the war was going against them. They recruited several high-ranking generals to become part of the conspiracy, led by Lieutenant Colonel Count Klaus von Stauffenberg, who had lost an eye, a hand, and two additional fingers on his other hand in combat, and who loathed Hitler.

Stauffenberg speedily put together a plot to assassinate Hitler and most of his loyal generals before the Allied position became so strong there would be no chance for a compromise. When summoned to a meeting at Hitler's East Prussian headquarters, Stauffenberg took a briefcase with a time bomb in it. Stauffenberg placed the briefcase underneath the table.

North American P-51D Mustang. (Maxwell Air Force Base Archives)

At half past noon, July 20, 1944, the bomb exploded. Four men were killed, twenty wounded. Hitler's life was spared by a heavy table that blocked the impact of the blast, but he was temporarily deafened and paralyzed in one arm, and also burned. Stauffenberg and the other conspirators were killed; thousands more—some innocent and others not—were rounded up, tried, sentenced, and hastily hanged. Their agony was filmed on Hitler's orders and shown to selected military audiences as a warning. Others committed suicide, among them Field Marshal Rommel, who was suspected of being a part of the conspiracy (though he was not). It was announced, however, that the popular and well-loved general had been killed in a car accident.

Although the details of Germany's internal problems were not generally known, many of the Allied soldiers felt instinctively that the enemy was weakening. They had Hitler on the run. And it showed in the growing confidence of the military units.

On July 12, 1944, Captain Joseph D. Elsberry from Langston, Oklahoma, became the first black pilot to score three kills in one day. Eight days later Elsberry scored his fourth victory while escorting B-24s of the 47th Bomber Wing in the Munich area. While in pursuit of still another enemy aircraft, he was forced to pull up to avoid running into a mountain peak. "This was the last time I engaged an enemy aircraft at close range," said Elsberry, "and my failure to register this victory meant the difference of being cited as an ace."

Soon after D-Day, the Allied forces had begun planning the invasion of southern France with a target date of August 15, 1944. Bolstered by the potential of a victory, the members of the 332nd participated in the preparations for the invasion. They accompanied B-24s from the 49th Bomber Wing in their attack on bridges at Theoule sur Mer and across the Var River. They provided fighter protection for the 55th on a mission to knock out railroad bridges at Avignon. And in several missions the black airmen destroyed radar stations on the coast of France.

Ground troops landed on August 15, and eight days later Paris was liberated.

The last day of the campaign had been costly for the 332nd. Several pilots had been lost, among them Lieutenant Alexander Jefferson, whose plane had been seen in flames, and Captain Robert H. Daniels, whose plane was also hit and seen spiraling into the ocean. The men held out hope that the pilots who crashed somehow survived and were being held as prisoners of war. In the case of Lieutenant Jefferson and Captain Daniels, that is exactly what happened.

Lieutenant Jefferson described his crash and capture during an interview years later: "I started my dive at 15,000 feet," he said,

General Dwight D. Eisenhower on D-Day. (NATIONAL AIR AND SPACE MUSEUM/SMITHSONIAN INSTITUTION)

"and went in straight for the station. But when I got about 200 yards from the target, a 20 mm shot burst through the floor of my cockpit. Immediately, my plane burst into flames. I kept my control, however, rolled my plane to the left, pushed forward on the stick, and fell out of my plane at about 600 feet. I landed about 200 feet from the target and was immediately picked up by the Germans and taken to the head-quarters of a flak battalion."

Captain Daniels's plane was hit by a 20mm shell that ripped it apart. His plane landed in the water, but somehow he managed to escape before it sank. The Germans pulled him from the water and brought him to where they were holding Jefferson. "Frankly," said Jefferson, "it made me feel much better to have someone I knew with me. You know, misery loves company."

Upon reaching Zagan, Germany, Daniels and Jefferson were separat-ed. Jefferson was taken to Stalag Luft III and Daniels was confined in Stalag Luft II.

Then came the interrogations. One POW, who was interviewed by television producer Tony Brown, recalled: "I expected to be treated badly. Instead I was treated like an officer. . . . I was amazed at how much [the German stalag commanders] knew about us [the Red Tails]. They opened a file that was full of information about our group." The black POWs were asked repeatedly why they would risk their lives for a country that didn't respect them as men.

According to Jefferson, there were ten officers who lived in a room about sixteen feet by sixteen feet. "We did our own cooking and made our own implements from cans received in Red Cross parcels. But in spite of the hardship of prison life the morale of the prisoners was rather high. Most of my roommates were Southerners. Two were from Georgia, three from Alabama, two from Florida, and one from Missouri and one from Michigan. Although I was a Negro they treated me as one of them. Each man performed a duty, and each day we combined our rations, cooked it together, and shared equally."

Meanwhile, during the rest of August 1944, the pilots of the 332nd continued to rack up victories. They battered German targets in strafing missions in Romania and Czechoslovakia and destroyed aircraft in the air and on the ground. On the twenty-seventh and thirtieth, they wiped out a total of twenty-two enemy aircraft confirmed by cameras mounted on the wings of the aircraft. They might have destroyed eighty or more, all on the ground, but it was hard to confirm ground hits because of the smoke and debris. In another raid they claimed twenty-two enemy airplanes, which, according to Rose, ranged "from Ju-87 Stukas (the terror of undefended skies earlier in the war), through Heinkel 111 medium bombers to Junkers 52 transports, plus one locomotive thrown in for good measure."

Three days later the 332nd repeated the performance in the Transylvania region of Romania. This time the planes included some of the best the Germans had to offer: Me-109s, Dornier 217s, FW-189s,

98

Air traffic controllers were important members of the ground crew of the 332nd. They helped pilots land in often difficult conditions. (LIBRARY OF CONGRESS, PRINTS AND PHOTOGRAPHS DIVISION, TONI FRISSELL COLLECTION)

Colonel Davis briefing his men before an important mission. (LIBRARY OF CONGRESS, PRINTS AND PHOTOGRAPHS DIVISION, TONI FRISSELL COLLECTION)

Bf-210s, and Bf-110s, for a total of eighty-three confirmed enemy aircraft. The intelligence officer of the 332nd reported: "Not a single enemy plane rose to meet them in an effort to stop the destruction. . . .

They were parked there like ducks, all we had to do was shoot them. . . . No matter how much pressure they are under, no excuse can be made for the Germans leaving so many planes concentrated in such large numbers. They must have lost all discipline."

Back home, black newspapers were filled with stories about the successes of the 332nd. Black war correspondents from the *Pittsburgh Courier*, the *Baltimore Afro-American*, and the *Norfolk Journal and Guide* covered the men in combat. According to Colonel Davis, "Black correspondents on the front asked for no special privileges. They endured the heat and cold. They lived with us in tents, along with the snakes and lizards. They ate C-rations and K-rations; they endured the mud and dust. The malaria-bearing mosquitoes bit them as well as us."

The stories that interested the readers back home were about how African-American soldiers were treated by European whites. Rest camps had been set up in Rome, Naples, and other cities, and they were visited frequently by black airmen, their crews, and black correspondents. Soon they began seeing signs all over Naples warning Italian women that black men were inferior beings and that any woman who dated a black man would be dishonored or killed. Mostly it was the work of disgruntled or jealous boyfriends, but some of the black soldiers believed that white soldiers had "planted the seeds of racism, and fascism did the rest."

Even so, morale among the 332nd was running high. Each man took pride in his mission performance. The Allies were gaining momentum, which made people hopeful that the war in Europe might end soon. And besides, the 332nd was finally getting the recognition it deserved. According to Colonel Davis, "Our pilots had become experts in bomber escort, and they knew it." It was a perfect time to honor members of their group.

On September 10, 1944, four pilots of the 332nd were presented the Distinguished Flying Cross. General Benjamin O. Davis, Sr., was in

General. B. O. Davis, Sr., pins the Distinguished Flying Cross on his son, Col. B. O. Davis, Jr., in September 1944. Others who were honored that same day were Capt. Joseph D. Elsberry, Lt. Jack Hosclaw, and Lt. Clarence Lester.
(NATIONAL AIR AND SPACE MUSEUM/SMITHSONIAN INSTITUTION)

Europe working on army promotional films. After completing their work in France, General Davis and the film detachment went to the Mediterranean theater of war, just in time for the general to proudly pin the Distinguished Flying Cross on his own son, Colonel Benjamin O. Davis, Jr., along with Captain Joseph D. Elsberry, First Lieutenant Jack D. Hosclaw, and First Lieutenant Clarence D. "Lucky" Lester.

The elder Davis told reporters afterward, "It was my happy privilege and good luck to be here for this grand occasion." One month later, his son was awarded the Legion of Merit, an award created by Congress in 1942. (Davis had known he was a recipient since March.)

THE RAINS CAME in September, and the month's death toll for the 332nd was the highest it had ever been. In a recent conversation, Captain Chris Newman, who in 1944 was a twenty-two-year-old second lieutenant and pilot of the *Goodwiggle*, remembered what it was like to take a hit and survive.

On September 22, 1944, Newman began a mission to Munich at about ten o'clock in the morning. Sixteen P-51s made up the squadron that day, along with two extras. The spares flew alongside the squadron so that if there was any trouble they could escort the troubled plane back to the base. "They were like spare tires," said Newman.

The flight plan took them over the Adriatic Sea, but at the northernmost point they picked up some flak from artillery shells. Newman was hit, and his engine started cutting out. Fire was coming from his engines. "I didn't want to go down in the Adriatic," said Newman, "because we'd already lost nine men in those waters. I just wanted to keep my

Black airmen who were injured were treated at a military hospital in Naples, Italy. (CHRIS NEWMAN PRIVATE COLLECTION)

plane up long enough to get to the coast. Then I could belly land on the beach." But fire was pouring out of his engines. He had to abandon his ship. Quickly, he pulled the cord that was supposed to unlatch the canopy, but it was stuck. So he unfastened the clip on the door, rolled the plane over, popped the stick forward, and he tumbled out.

"I was out in space, falling out of control," Newman said. "Then I remembered in training we were told to snap to attention." He did, and he straightened up. As precious seconds ticked away, Newman pulled what he thought was his parachute rip cord. But his chute didn't open. "I was about to panic," he said, "but then I realized I had my oxygen cord in my hand instead of my chute ring." He found the rip cord, pulled it, and the chute opened. He landed in the water safely and inflated the small water raft that was part of his emergency pack. Then he marked the waters around him with the can of yellow dye in his pack. "I was wet but alive." Lieutenant Newman was picked up several hours later.

The weather cleared up about mid-October. By that time the Germans were on the defensive, retreating farther into Germany, where they were preparing to make their last stand. Intelligence reported that the Germans were saving their best pilots for the defense of their own country, but the Allied air forces were ready for their challenge.

The 332nd was sent to strafe traffic on the Danube River. Lee "Buddy" Archer was flying wingman for the flamboyant Wendell Pruitt. Archer had already scored two victories. Pruitt went after an enemy He-111 medium bomber. Seven Me-109s and two more He-111s appeared out of the clouds and attacked Pruitt from his lower-left side. Lieutenant Archer described the dogfight: "We had just crossed Lake Balaton, when I spied a group of enemy aircraft at two o'clock high and climbing. Two Messerschmitts were flying abreast. I tore the wing off one with a long burst. The other slid in behind Pruitt. I pulled up, zeroed in, hit the gun button, and watched him explode."

Captain Andrew D. Turner (l), commanding officer of the 100th Fighter Squadron, congratulating Lt. Clarence "Lucky" Lester (r), who had three enemy kills to his credit. (NATIONAL AIR AND SPACE MUSEUM/SMITHSONIAN INSTITUTION)

Lieutenant Lee "Buddy" Archer, member of the 302nd Fighter Squadron, is often remembered as "one of the best." (NATIONAL AIR AND SPACE MUSEUM/SMITHSONIAN INSTITUTION)

Pruitt was chasing an enemy aircraft when his guns jammed. Archer followed the enemy aircraft as it took a sharp dive. "I don't know whether he was damaged by Pruitt or not," said Archer, "but he appeared to be trying to land. I opened up at ground level, hit him with a long volley and he crashed. Flak and small arms fire forced me out of there in a hurry."

Archer had four confirmed victories and one maybe. Many people thought that Archer had scored the five to become the only ace among the pilots of the 332nd. But the last kill became controversial because it wasn't clear whether Pruitt had hit the enemy first or if Archer had. In a few records, Archer is listed as an ace, but in official air force records he is not included.

There were nine victories that day with only one loss. "We lost a lot of good men," said Lester. "When I say a lot, one is too many."

It was difficult for some of the men to cope with the idea that they were killing people. Louis Purnell (then a lieutenant) described what it felt like to realize he had taken another human being's life.

> After returning to the base [after a strafing mission] I checked the aircraft—a brand new P-51 on its maiden combat mission—for bullet holes. Hanging over the edge of the airscoop beneath the place was a strange object—a black-brownish glob, wet in some spots. I poked at it with a stick, and it fell to the ground. . . . Then it dawned on me: this was part of a man. . . . My first thought was *better he than me* but then I started thinking seriously about what had happened. Eighty minutes ago that man was alive and healthy, and whole. His parents had raised him just as mine had raised me. He had nothing against me and I had nothing against him, but since our countries were at war, killing was legal. When called to arms, one must defend his country . . . but it all seemed so futile.

In time Marchbank (who had been promoted to major) expanded his psychological program to include evaluations. A total of 285 pilots were assigned to the 332nd Fighter Group between February 1944 and February 1945, but only two were discharged because of psychiatric reasons.

When bomber pilots saw the Red Tails, they relaxed. The pilots of the 332nd had a reputation for staying with the bombers they escorted, rather than leaving them to chalk up kills for their own personal glory. For this reason they became known as the Red-Tail Angels. It is a matter of record: the pilots of the 332nd never lost a bomber they were escorting. No other group in the United States Army Air Forces could make that claim.

There were those who were so blinded by their own racism that they could not bring themselves to acknowledge the accomplishments of the black pilots. Purnell (who is now a captain) illustrates that point in a story that happened around Christmas 1944. "Bad weather had forced the bombers we were escorting to land at our base. I was serving as the base censor, which meant I had to read all the out-going mail to make sure there was nothing the enemy could use if the letters were confiscated. I came across one letter I must have read fifty times: 'Dearest . . . My heart bleeds that I'm not with you at Christmas. . . . It's bad enough I'm not on my own base. I'm stranded at a nigger base, eating nigger food, and sleeping in a nigger bed.'"

The next day, as the bomber crew and the escort squadrons were beginning to assemble for takeoff, Purnell located the white bomber crewman. "Sergeant," he said, "it wasn't so bad sleeping in nigger beds and eating nigger food, especially when we protect you in flight. I'll see you up there." Purnell walked away without bothering to wait for a response.

It was about this time the Germans introduced jet aircraft into combat with their Messerschmitt 262 (Me-262). It could fly well over five hundred miles per hour, a full hundred miles faster than the best

A German Messerschmitt 109G-6l R6, one of the fighter planes designed by Willy Messerschmitt. (MAXWELL AIR FORCE BASE ARCHIVES)

Allied propeller-driven fighters, and even a little faster than a British-built jet fighter that was also introduced. During the month of December the 332nd flew twenty-three missions and finally caught its first glimpse of the German fighter jets.

Seeing one for the first time, a pilot said, "It flew past us so fast, we never got a chance to call it in."

Many historians believe Germany's defeat was due in part to several poor decisions made by Hitler and his high command regarding jet air-craft development. Jet engine development had been taking place in England, the United States, and Germany since 1918, and several pro-totypes had been built.

It was Willy Messerschmitt's Me-262 jet fighter that could have been a very powerful weapon in the hands of the Germans had they understood its potential. But Erhard Milch, a high-ranking Nazi officer, head of Lufthansa, and in charge of all machine purchases, had a per-sonal grudge against Messerschmitt.

Willy Messerschmitt, born in 1898, the son of a Frankfurt wine merchant, had been obsessed with aviation since early childhood. With the help of a friend, Messerschmitt began building gliders and later airplanes.

In 1931, two M-20s built by Messerschmitt crashed, killing a personal friend of Erhard Milch. He blamed Messerschmitt for the accident and never forgave him. In 1940, Hitler's close advisors, following his orders, decreed that "no research or development should be pursued unless it promised military results within four months." As a result of this shortsighted decision, all work on Messerschmitt's Me-262 jet fighter was forbidden. However, Messerschmitt continued to work on his design. When Milch found out about it in the spring of 1941, he went to Messerschmitt's home and insisted that he stop working on the jet.

War historians believe those orders delayed the Me-262 by about two years, which gave the Allies an advantage. By the time the Me-262 was approved and built, it was simply too little too late.

The 332nd pilots would engage Me-262s in the air later. But for the moment it was time to celebrate Christmas, read mail from home, open packages, show off pictures, and hope for an end to the war in the coming year. In his year-end message to his men, Colonel Davis said:

> I cannot fail to mention the all-important fact that your achievements have been recognized. Unofficially you are known by an untold number of bomber crews as those who can be depended upon and whose appearance means certain protection from enemy fighters. The bomber crews have told others of your accomplishments, and your good reputation has preceded you in many parts where you may think you are unknown. The Commanding General of the Fifteenth Fighter Command has stated that we are doing a good job and thus, the official report of our operations is a creditable one.

108

seven
1945

REBELLION IN THE RANKS

BACK IN THE United States, the Army Air Force had established the all-black 477th Bombardment Group at about the same time the 332nd Fighter Group had been formed. Stationed first at Selfridge Field near

The ground crew of the 332nd Fighter Group was important. The planes required expert mechanics to keep them running. (L to R) Sgts. Calvin Thierry, prop specialist; William Pitts, engine specialist; Vernon Richardson, engine specialist, and Harold Cobb, crew chief. (NATIONAL AIR AND SPACE MUSEUM/SMITHSONIAN INSTITUTION)

Detroit, the 477th was a particularly tense organization because the facilities were too crowded and racism was widespread.

When a black officer applied for membership in the all-white officers' club, General Frank Hunter, commander of the 1st Air Force at Mitchell Field, New York, visited Selfridge. "As long as I am commander of the 1st Air Force, there will be no racial mixing at any post under my command. There are no racial problems on this base and there will be none!" In an official report he blamed outside agitation that had made "his Negroes 'surly.'"

Hoping to offset unrest among the black officers, Congress appropriated seventy-five thousand dollars to build a "black officers' club," but the 477th was transferred to Godman Field near Fort Knox, Kentucky before its officers ever got to use it. Then, on March 15, 1945, the unit moved to a base ironically named Freeman Field, located in Seymour, Indiana, near Fort Knox.

Freeman Field, commanded by Colonel Robert Selway, was anything but free for the blacks who were stationed there. There were 400 black officers and 2,500 enlisted men compared to 250 white officers and 600 enlisted men on base. Blacks weren't in charge of anything. And, to make matters worse, the base segregation policies were rigidly enforced.

Officers' Club 1 was for the African-Americans. The men called it Uncle Tom's Cabin. Officers' Club 2 was reserved for whites and was considered off-limits to blacks regardless of their rank.

After discussing their outrage at the treatment they were receiving, several black soldiers decided to protest. On the evening of April 5, 1945, an incident occurred unparalleled in army history. At about 9:15 P.M., a group of black officers, all pilots with several years of experience, asked for entry into the white-only club at the base. Their request was denied.

Within the hour, another group tried to enter, led by Lieutenant

Marsden Thompson, who politely stated that he wanted to exercise his privileges as an officer of the United States Army Air Corps and enter the club for a drink. When his request was denied, Thompson brushed past the officer on duty, and all the men behind him filed in without using physical force. Later that evening, Lieutenant Robert Terry used the same method to gain entry.

By the next evening, over sixty black officers were arrested, and on April 9, 1945, a new regulation for the base was released: *Assignment of Housing, Messing and Recreational Facilities for Officers, Flight Officers and Warrant Officers*, known as Regulation 85-2. Authored by General Hunter and Colonel Selway, the regulation specified the strict segregation of housing, dining halls, and officers' clubs, and added that "any insubordination regarding racial mixing would be met by confinement to the guard house."

Colonel Selway called all the black officers together—even those who hadn't participated in the demonstration—and ordered them to sign a statement that they had read Regulation 85-2 and accepted the conditions of the policy. One hundred and one black officers refused to sign the document.

The officers of the 477th had been angered by army regulations at Selfridge, Godman, and Freeman that insisted upon keeping the races separate, even in movie theaters on bases. General Hunter instructed the women in the Women's Air Corps (WACs), who were all white at the time, not to associate with blacks on or off base. (According to records, there was never a reported rape or assault on any female personnel—white or black—at Tuskegee Army Air Field during the time it was open.) Adding to the problems of discrimination were incidents of beatings and shootings. In 1943 an intoxicated white officer shot and wounded a black soldier without provocation, and no punitive actions were taken against the officer.

When word of what was happening spread, the men were ready to take action. They thought of ways they could help those who had been arrested. Some of the men were concerned that the army would use the incident to portray blacks as deserters or traitors. Would they be court-martialed and dishonorably discharged from the army just like the soldiers in the Brownsville Case (see pages 7–8)? Knowing the history of the military's action toward demonstrations against its authority, a majority of the men still agreed that in unity they were strong.

In the midst of the controversy, President Roosevelt died unexpectedly on April 12, 1945. The nation took time to mourn.

Finally, on April 19th, the dissident officers were released, except for the three men who were involved in the initial confrontations at the clubs.

Several men emerged from this episode as leaders: William Coleman, who would one day serve as secretary of transportation under President Gerald Ford, and Coleman Young, who would later become

The leadership qualities that Chappie James exhibited early in his career led to his continuing military successes as a pilot in Korea and Southeast Asia. (THE UNITED STATES AIRFORCE MUSEUM, DAYTON, OHIO)

mayor of Detroit, made their contributions outside the military. A young officer named Daniel "Chappie" James remained in the military and would one day become a four-star general in the United States Air Force.

Born in Pensacola, Florida, in 1920, Chappie James was the youngest of seventeen children. Although he was dismissed from Tuskegee Institute for fighting, he quickly turned his life around by joining the Army Air Corps at TAAF. He was commissioned a second lieutenant at TAAF in July 1943. While stationed at Selfridge Field, he was reassigned to the 477th Bombardment Group and trained in medium-range, multi-engine bombers (B-25s).

Chappie, who had been described as "headstrong, irreverent, and mischievous," was always looking for ways to circumvent ridiculous rules regarding segregation. He had been adamant about not signing Regulation 85-2. He was arrested, but soon released because the army needed him to fly orders to and from Washington. Using the freedom he was given, Chappie helped his friends by serving as a courier, taking messages written by Coleman and Young to the "outside world."

Because of the pressure put on the War Department by civil rights organizations and the black press, Stimson ordered the McCloy Committee to investigate illegal segregation in the army. After a quick review of the facts, Stimson specifically declared in Regulation 210-10 that "no longer could separation of military personnel be based on race in the use of facilities, including officers' clubs."

Colonel Robert Selway was removed as commander of the 477th for losing control and allowing the mutiny. General Hunter, who accepted no blame, insisted that the War Department took orders from Eleanor Roosevelt. Lieutenants Thompson and Terry, who were still being held, were fined one hundred fifty dollars and then released.

The 477th had won a small victory for civil rights in the United States. Meanwhile black pilots were still in combat in Europe.

DURING THE FIRST few months of 1945, Russian Allies were forging ahead in the Balkans. In three weeks they pushed the Germans back 272 miles from Warsaw, Poland, to Frankfurt, Germany.

German oil resources had been depleted by the Allies' air offensive. German transportation and communication systems had been disrupted, and German troops were completely demoralized. On the western front, the Americans and British were planning an attack across the Rhine. It was a just a matter of time before Germany's defeat.

One of the concerns the Allied air forces had was Germany's jet aircraft development. In late 1944 and early 1945, squadrons were encountering both the Me-262 and the new Me-163. The 163 was a rocket-propelled single-seated fighter. It could climb fast but had limited endurance. If the Germans succeeded in putting a large number of jets in the air, they could prolong the war. The Allies decided to bomb Nazi aircraft factories. Wherever the 15th Air Force bombers flew, the 332nd squadrons acted as escort, and they strafed enemy troops and supplies along the way.

The last few months of the war in Germany as seen through the eyes of a POW were "almost agony." Lieutenant Alexander Jefferson, who had been a prisoner since August of 1944, said that in spite of what the Germans told them, the POWs suspected the Germans were losing the war. "We knew the Americans were coming," said Jefferson, "and feared the Germans might shoot us rather than let us be rescued by the Allies. We also feared that we would be caught in the midst of a battle. . . . We watched B-17s bomb Munich one day. It was really a wonderful sight, but after that we feared that we would be victims of such a raid."

During the last week in March, Colonel Davis led the 332nd on a sixteen-hundred-mile round-trip mission to Berlin, providing cover for B-17 bombers. It was recorded as one of the longest missions in 15th Air Force history. The objective: to bomb the Daimler Benz Tank

(L to R) Line Chief Sergeant Charley Haynes along with Sgts. James Sheppard and Frank Bradley install extra large external gas tanks in the planes of the 332nd, for a special mission from Southern Italy to Berlin, the longest mission in the war. (MAXWELL AIR FORCE BASE ARCHIVES)

(L to R) Sergeant Richard Adams, Capt. Armour McDaniel, Lt. James McFatridge, and Lt. Ulysses Taylor inspect flak damage to Capt. McDaniel's fighter. (Capt. McDaniel was later taken as a POW after surviving a crash landing.) (MAXWELL AIR FORCE BASE ARCHIVES)

Works. The mission plan was for the 332nd to relieve the AP-38 Fighter Group and take the bombers to the outskirts of Berlin. There the 332nd was supposed to be relieved by another fighter group. But when they got to the destination, the Red Tails were told to stay with the bombers.

Colonel Davis's Mustang *Bennie* developed trouble, which forced him to return to base, leaving Captain Armour McDaniel in command. Over the target the 332nd encountered the new German jet planes for the first time in combat. Although their machines were superior, Luftwaffe pilots were only receiving one-third the training American and British pilots were getting. Their inexperience was evident during confrontations against seasoned pilots who understood their airplanes. This may account for the success of the Red Tails, who scored victories against the German jets.

The 332nd Fighter Group was awarded the Distinguished Unit Citation for successfully escorting the bombers and for their outstanding and aggressive combat techniques during this mission.

But the 332nd didn't rest on its laurels. On March 31, 1945, the Red Tails were sent on a strafing mission near Linz, Austria, where they encountered seventeen Messerschmitt 262s and Focke-Wulfs. They shot down thirteen of them without a loss to themselves.

In the midst of its battles, the 332nd received word that President Roosevelt, the group's commander in chief, had died. Vice President Harry S Truman, a Missourian, became president. While the pilots of the 332nd mourned the loss of their president, they also mourned the loss of one of their own, Captain Wendell O. Pruitt.

Pruitt, who had completed seventy combat missions and was awarded the Distinguished Flying Cross and the Air Medal with six oak-leaf clusters (meaning he had won the medal at least six times), had returned to TAAF to become a trainer. He was unhappy with the assignment and wrote Colonel Davis, requesting to return to the front.

116

Captain Wendell Pruitt (l) with crew chief Samuel W. Jacobs (r). (NATIONAL AIR
AND SPACE MUSEUM/SMITHSONIAN INSTITUTION)

General Davis was planning to recall Pruitt when news arrived that
Pruitt had been killed in a training crash.

The priest who eulogized him said, "Captain Pruitt is dead, but the
fruits of his life will be multiplied over the earth. He was a student, a
man who used his intellectual abilities to achieve. All of us could learn
from Wendell Pruitt the necessity of labor to accomplish our goal.
We needed a modern hero for us to pattern our lives so God called
him home."

Captain Chris Newman said of Wendell Pruitt, "He was without a
doubt one of the best we had in the skies at that time. On the ground
Pruitt was a quiet, unassuming man. He just flew loud."

ON APRIL 15, Colonel Davis led his group on a difficult strafing mission over Austria. They racked up an astonishing thirty-five locomotives, fifty-two rail vehicles, four barges, and four motor vehicles. A few days later, the 332nd escorted B-24 bombers of the 55th and 304th Bomber Wings over northern Italy, during which they destroyed four enemy aircraft in the Mediterranean. The group flew its final mission on April 30, 1945.

The war ended in Europe on May 8, 1945.

The 332nd's combat record was impressive, and its pilots were rewarded with Distinguished Flying Crosses, a Legion of Merit, a silver star, eight purple hearts, and over 744 Air Medals and clusters. Formal recognition was given to the men on May 11.

Although the war in Europe was over, the war in the Pacific was still going on. The men of the 332nd wondered if they'd be sent to fight the Japanese.

In June 1945, Colonel Davis was named the commander of the 477th Composite Group. By assuming command of Godman Field on July 1, Colonel Davis made the record books with another first in Army Air Force history. The 477th consisted of two medium-size bombardment squadrons, which would include the 99th and the 100th Fighter Squadrons.

Colonel Davis selected his own staff. It was the first time all responsible positions were held by blacks. Among his officers were men who had served under him in Europe. The commander of the revised 99th Fighter Squadron, Major William Campbell, was a veteran of 106 combat missions and the recipient of the Distinguished Flying Cross with nine oak-leaf clusters. Davis also appointed his long-time friend, Major Vance Marchbank, as the flight surgeon. Marchbank was later to become a general.

118

Lieutenant Clarence Lester wearing his Distinguished Flying Cross.
(CHRIS NEWMAN PRIVATE COLLECTION)

The Composite Group underwent intensive tactical training for participation in the Pacific theater, but the war ended before they were called up for action.

President Truman, along with Winston Churchill and Joseph Stalin, issued the Potsdam Declaration in July 1945 demanding Japan's unconditional surrender. When Japan refused, the United States dropped the first atomic bomb on the Japanese city of Hiroshima, August 6, 1945. It destroyed 60 percent of the city and killed or injured more than seventy thousand people. Two days later, Stalin declared war on Japan and launched a powerful offensive against Japanese forces in Manchuria. Japan still refused to accept the unconditional surrender. On August 9, 1945, a second bomb was released on Nagasaki. Forty thousand more died. The Japanese surrender was negotiated between August 10 and August 14, 1945, ending World War II.

Colonel Edward C. Gleed (retired), one of the most decorated pilots in the 332nd, summarized the feelings of pilots and crew members who had participated in the Tuskegee "experiment": "When we were training at Tuskegee and in combat, we never gave it a thought that we were making history. All we wanted was to learn how to fly as Army Air Corps pilots, fight for our country, and survive." And that's what they had done.

EPILOGUE
1946–1948

AFTER THE WAR, the black squadrons of the 332nd were deactivated, and some of the men were sent to Godman Field under Davis's command. But others were sent back to Tuskegee.

Tuskegee had become a white elephant to the Army Air Force. Conditions there were overcrowded and tense. Hundreds of capable officers had nothing to do. "The Army didn't know what to do with all these black officers they had trained," a returning pilot said, expressing the frustration he felt. "We felt pushed aside, out of sight, out of mind. Our personal sacrifices seemed meaningless!"

Many of the men concluded that the army didn't need or want them. And after several of the black squadrons were deactivated, many of them left the service.

Unfortunately, black servicemen weren't embraced by the civilian community either. The NAACP reported that 1946 was "one of the grimmest years in the history of the organization." There was a wave of lynchings and reports of blowtorch killings and eye-gouging of black veterans. Where were the promises of postwar equality and decency?

For those who stayed in the service, there was a period of adjustment from a wartime military to a peacetime military. In March 1946, the 477th Composite Group moved to Lockbourne Field in Columbus,

Ohio. When news reached the city that the unit was coming, there was a general cry of outrage. The editor of the *Columbus Citizen* wrote in an editorial: "The 477th were a bunch of troublemakers." But the black people of Columbus found out when the 477th was coming, and they lined the streets to cheer and welcome its men to their new home.

After only two months at Lockbourne, the Composite Group was deactivitated and the 332nd Fighter Group was reactivated. A few months later, the group became the 332nd Fighter Wing, and the manpower was reduced to about one hundred pilots. The ground personnel included about seventeen hundred people, including detachments of Women of the Air Force (WAF).

It was at Godman and Lockbourne that Colonel Davis encountered Chappie James, who had reenlisted in the military. About the only thing the two men had in common was their iron-willed determination to succeed. Davis's formal command style and Chappie's easy-going manner collided head-on.

Many years later when both men were generals, James gave Davis this compliment: "General Davis had a job to do, and if he hadn't held tight rein . . . that unit would have been taken away from him." According to one James biographer, J. Alfred Phelps, "if [General] Davis had not held a tight rein over Chappie (and the rest), the odds are that Chappie never

General Benjamin O. Davis, Jr., retired. (The United States Air Force Museum, Dayton, Ohio)

122

President Harry Truman withstood criticism from his political and military advisers in order to desegregate the U.S. armed forces. (LIBRARY OF CONGRESS)

General Daniel "Chappie" James became the first black four-star general in the United States. (NATIONAL AIR AND SPACE MUSEUM/SMITHSONIAN INSTITUTION)

would have survived his own expansive temperament to become a four-star general."

Other Tuskegee Airmen remained in the service, became officers, and served in Korea and Vietnam.

Some historians believe the outstanding performance records of the 99th Fighter Squadron, the 332nd Fighter Group, and the 477th Bombardment and Composite Groups helped bring an end to segregation in the army.

Following the war, the U.S. government realized that it needed to extend constitutional guarantees to all its citizens, especially if it was going to be a credible leader of the free world. President Harry S Truman decided that the federal government could no longer condone or maintain a segregated military. Using his power as commander in chief of the armed forces, the president issued Executive Order 9981 on July 26, 1948. It stated in part:

> It is hereby declared to be the policy of the President that there
> shall be equality of treatment and opportunity for all persons in
> the armed services without regard to race, color, religion, or
> national origin. This policy shall be put into effect as rapidly as
> possible, having due regard to the time required to effectuate
> any necessary changes without impairing efficiency or morale.

The terminology in the executive order caused a heated debate about its interpretation. Nowhere in the statement was there mention of an end to segregation. Segregationists often used the term *equality of treatment and opportunity* when justifying the "separate but equal" doctrine of apartheid. Blacks were also familiar with the language and called for clarity. Then General Omar Bradley, the army's chief of staff, further clouded the issue. Responding to a reporter's question without

The legacy of the Tuskegee Airmen lives on through the accomplishments of African-Americans in the space program such as the ones featured here: (l to r) Guion Bluford (USAF), Ronald McNair, Ph.D., Fredrick Gregory (USAF), Charles Bolden (USMC). (THE UNITED STATES AIR FORCE MUSEUM, DAYTON, OHIO)

having read the president's order, Bradley said "the Army was no place to conduct social experiments" and that desegregation would come to the Army only "when it was a fact in the rest of the United States."

The press inferred that Bradley and the military were prepared to resist the president's order. Southerners held Bradley up as a national hero. Bradley, of course, wrote the president, apologizing for the statement, which he said had been taken out of context. He vowed to carry out the president's order to the letter.

President Truman held a press conference during which he clearly stated that the armed forces were to be integrated immediately. By 1947, the Army Air Force had become the United States Air Force and had begun its own desegregation policies led by Lieutenant General I. E. Edwards, who was the air force's deputy chief of staff for personnel.

Edwards had served on the McCloy Committee and was aware of the waste of manpower that resulted from the army's segregation policy.

Eventually segregation was eliminated from all branches of the military forces. Today it is difficult to conceive that an "experiment" was needed to prove that African-Americans are as capable as whites, especially in view of General Colin Powell, former chairman of the Joint Chiefs of Staff; the black astronauts (men and women); and the veterans of Korea, Vietnam, and the Persian Gulf, all of whom have made outstanding contributions in military service. The army didn't know it at the time, but they had produced in the Tuskegee Airmen a powerful force that, indeed, worked to destroy the racial barriers the military and the nation were so reluctant to pull down on their own.

Above all, let us never forget
that they saw opportunity
and they took it, breaking
through past bonds into flight.
Pilots they were, and good ones.
Men who lived with courage, joy,
enduring that despair imposed
by the limits of others.

Those in any vanguard
carry the abusing gift
of the foresight of God.
Who pities Joan of Arc?
Or sees Moses or Dr. King
as underprivileged?

—Carol Washburne, 1994

APPENDIX

COMBAT RECORD OF BLACK AIRMEN AS OF JUNE 9, 1945

	Destroyed	Damaged	Total
Aircraft (aerial)	111	25	136
Aircraft (ground)	150	123	273
Barges and boats	16	24	40
Boxcars, other rolling stock	58	561	619
Buildings and factories	0	23	23
Gun emplacements	3	0	3
Destroyers	1	0	1
Horse-drawn vehicles	15	100	115
Locomotives	57	69	126
Motor transports	6	81	87
Oil and ammunition dumps	2	0	2
Power transformers	3	2	5
Radar installations	1	8	9
Tanks on flat cars	0	7	7
Total missions of 12th Air Force			1,267
Total missions of 15th Air Force			311
Total sorties of 12th Air Force			6,381
Total sorties of 15th Air Force			9,152
Grand total, missions			1,578
Grand total, sorties			15,533
Total number of pilots sent overseas			450
Total number of pilots graduated at Tuskegee			993
Awards			
Legion of Merit			1
Silver Star			1
Soldier Medal			2
Purple Heart			8
Distinguished Flying Cross *			95
Bronze Star			14
Air Medal and Clusters			744

* (Charles E. Francis, in *The Tuskegee Airmen* [1988], estimates the total number of Distinguished Flying Crosses awarded to black pilots at 150.)

are classified by both letters and numbers. The letters tell the
… the numbers designate the model. If more than one letter is
… letter shows the current modification, and the second letter
… design.

	P—Patrol
	Q—Target and drone
… transport	R—Reconnaissance
	S—Antisubmarine
	SR—Strategic Reconnaissance
…	TR—Tactical Reconnaissance
	T—Trainer
… arrier	U—Utility
… on	X—Experimental

GLOSSARY
OF ARMY AIR FORCE
UNITS DURING
WORLD WAR II

…he smallest unit in the Army Air Force. There
…ly four fighters in a flight.

…*dron*—Squadrons were composed of four or more

…—During World War II, most fighter groups were com-
…e fighter squadrons. (See chart on p. 93.)

…*Force*—Consisted of three or more fighter groups.

… The air corps was a command within the U.S. Army
…rld War II.

…*artment*—Under the direction of the secretary of
…e war department was a nonmilitary cabinet

U.S. AIR FORCE INSIGNIA
INSIGNIA FOR OFFICERS

Second Lieutenant (silver)	
First Lieutenant (gold)	
Captain	
Major (silver)	
Lieutenant Colonel (gold)	
Colonel	
Brigadier General	
Major General	
Lieutenant General	
General	
General of the Air Force	

INSIGNIA FOR ENLISTED
PERSONNEL

Airman	
Airman First Class	
Senior Airman Sergeant	
Staff Sergeant	
Technical Sergeant	
Master Sergeant	
Senior Master Sergeant	

BIBLIOGRAPHY

Ambrose, Stephen. *Handbook on German Military Forces*. Baton Rouge, La: Louisiana State University Press,1990.

Applegate, Katherine. *The Story of Two American Generals: Colin Powell and Benjamin O. Davis*. New York: Dell, 1992.

Apthekers, Herbert. *A Documentary History of the Negro People in the United States*. Vol. 1. Secaucus, N. J.: Carol Publishing, 1993.

———. *A Documentary History of the Negro People in the United States*. Vol. 2. New York: Carol Publishing, 1951.

———. *A Documentary History of the Negro People in the United States*. Vol. 6. Secaucus, N.J.: Carol Publishing, 1993.

Asante, Molefi, and Mark Mattson. *Historical and Cultural Atlas of African Americans*. New York: Macmillan, 1992.

Bennett, Lerone. *A History of Black America*. Chicago, Ill.: Johnson Publishing, 1987.

Binkin, Martin, and Mark Eitelberg, with Alvin J. Schexnider and Marvin M. Smith. *Blacks and the Military*. Washington, D.C.: Brookings Institution, 1982.

Cornish, Taylor. *The Sable Arm Black Troops in the Union Army, 1861–1865*. Lawrence, Kans. University of Kansas Press, 1987.

Dabbs, Henry. *Black Brass.*Freehold, N.J.: Afro-American Heritage House, 1983.

Dalfiume, Richard. *Desegregation of the Armed Forces*. Columbia, Mo.: University of Missouri Press, 1960.

Davis, Burke. *Black Heroes of the American Revolution*. San Diego, Calif.: Harcourt Brace Jovanovich, 1967.

Drake, St. Clair, and Horace R. Clayton. *Black Metropolis: A Study of Negro Life in a Northern City*. Chicago, Ill.: University of Chicago Press, 1945.

Emert, Phyllis. *Fighter Planes*. Englewood Cliffs, N.J.: RGA Publishing Group, 1990.

Ferrell, Nancy. *The U.S. Air Force*. Minneapolis, Minn.: Lerner Publications, 1990.

Fletcher, Marvin. *America's First Black General, Benjamin O. Davis, Sr., 1880–1970*. Lawrence, Kans.: University of Kansas Press, 1989.

———. *The Black Soldier and Officer in the United States Army*. Columbia, Mo.: University of Missouri Press, 1974.

Francis, Charles. *The Tuskegee Airmen*. Boston, Mass.: Branden Publishing, 1987.

Gladstone, William. *United States Colored Troops,1863–1867*. Gettysburgh, Pa.: Thomas Publications, 1990.

Gurney, Gene. *Flying Aces of World War Two.* New York: Scholastic Book Services, 1965.

Hardesty, Von, and Dominick Pisano. *Black Wings.* Washington, D.C.: Smithsonian, 1984.

Hayden, Kate. *The Aircraft Encyclopedia.* New York: Simon & Schuster, 1985.

Herschler, Mildred. *The Walk into the Morning.* New York: Tom Doherty Associates, 1993.

Hole, Dorothy. *The Air Force and You.* New York: Crestwood House, 1993.

Hope, John, and Alfred Moss. *From Slavery to Freedom.* New York: McGraw-Hill, 1988.

Hornsby, Alton. *African American History.* Detroit: Gale Research, 1991.

Jakeman, Robert. *Divided Skies.* Tuscaloosa, Ala.: University of Alabama Press, 1992.

James, C. L. R. *Fighting Racism in World War Two.* New York: Anchor Foundation, 1980.

Katz, William. *The Colored Cadet at West Point.* Salem, N. H.: Ayer, 1986.

MacCloskey, Monro. *The United States Air Force.* New York: Praeger, 1967.

McGovern, James. *Black Eagle, General Daniel Chappie James, Jr.* Tuscaloosa, Ala.: University of Alabama Press, 1985.

Miller, Donald. *Blacks in the Armed Forces.* New York: Franklin Watts, 1969.

Moolman, Valerie. *Women Aloft.* Alexandria, Va.: Time Life Books, 1981.

Mullen, Robert. *Blacks in America's Wars.* New York: Anchor Foundation, 1973.

Nalty, Bernard. *Strength for the Fight.* London: Free Press, 1986.

Park, Edwards. *Fighters: The World's Great Aces and Their Planes.* Charlottesville, Va.: Thomasson-Grant, 1990.

Peterson, David. *Airplanes.* Chicago, Ill.: Children's Press, 1981.

Phelps, Alfred. *They Had a Dream: The Story of African-American Astronauts.* Navato, Calif.: Presidio Press, 1994.

Potter, Lou, with Miles Williams and Nina Rosenblum. *Liberators.* New York: Harcourt Brace Jovanovich Publishers, 1992.

Quarles, Benjamin. *The Negro in the Civil War.* New York: Da Capo Press, 1953.

Sterling, Dorothy. *The Trouble They Seen: The Story of Reconstruction in the Words of African-Americans.* New York: Da Capo Press, 1994.

Warnock, Timothy. *Combat Medals, Streamers, and Campaigns.* Washington, D.C.: United States Air Force Historical Research Center, 1990.

Weidenfeld, George. *Encyclopedia of Aircrafts.* New York: Putnam, 1978.

Welsh, Douglas. *The U.S.A. in World War Two.* New York: Gallery Books, 1982.

FILMS

Tony Brown's Journal (Shows 605–628). Producer and director, Tony Brown. Tony Brown Productions. Four videocassettes.

PERSONAL INTERVIEWS

Davis, Jr., Benjamin O., and other members of the Hugh White Chapter of the Tuskegee Airmen. With Patricia and Fredrick McKissack. St. Louis, Missouri, April 1993.

Newman, Chris, historian of the Hugh White Chapter of the Tuskegee Airmen. With Fredrick and Patricia McKissack. St. Louis, Missouri, May 1994, November 1994.

TELEPHONE INTERVIEWS

Mitchell, George. Tuskegee Air Base communications instructor. With Patricia McKissack, June 1994.

Caver, Joe, Archivist, Maxwell Air Force Base Research Center. With Fredrick McKissack, October 1994.

Crockett, Woodrow, former Tuskegee Airman, and a member of the Arkansas Hall of Fame. With Patricia McKissack, February 1995.

BIBLIOGRAPHY

133